Anita Brookner

Twayne's English Authors Series

Kinley E. Roby, Editor

Northeastern University

TEAS 473

Anita Brookner

By Lynn Veach Sadler

Methodist College

Twayne Publishers
A Division of G.K. Hall & Co. • *Boston*

Anita Brookner
Lynn Veach Sadler

Copyright 1990 by G. K. Hall & Co.
All rights reserved.
Published by Twayne Publishers
A Division of G. K. Hall & Co.
70 Lincoln Street
Boston, Massachusetts 02111

Copyediting supervised by Barbara Sutton
Book production by Gabrielle B. McDonald
Book design by Barbara Anderson

Typeset in 11 pt. Garamond
by Huron Valley Graphics, Inc., of Ann Arbor, Michigan

Printed on permanent/durable acid-free paper
and bound in the United States of America

First printed 1990
10 9 8 7 6 5 4 3 2 1

Library of Congress Cataloging-in-Publication Data

Sadler, Lynn Veach.
    Anita Brookner / by Lynn Veach Sadler.
        p.   cm. — (Twayne's English authors series : TEAS 473)
    Includes bibliographical references.
    Includes Index.
    ISBN 0-8057-6991-9 (alk. paper)
    1. Brookner, Anita—Criticism and interpretation.   I. Title.
    II. Series.
    PR6052.R5816Z87   1990
    823'.914—dc20   89-39237
                                                                  CIP

Contents

About the Author

Lynn Veach Sadler is vice president for academic affairs at Methodist College, Fayetteville, North Carolina. She received a B.A. from Duke University and an M.A. and a Ph.D. from the University of Illinois at Champaign-Urbana. A Miltonist, she has published books on John Milton, John Bunyan, Thomas Carew, and Margaret Drabble and over fifty articles. She has taught at Agnes Scott College, Drake University, A&T State University, and Bennett College, where she was director of the Division of Humanities. She won an Extraordinary Undergraduate Teaching Award at Drake University, was a panelist at the First International Milton Symposium in England, and has directed a National Endowment for the Humanities Summer Seminar for College Teachers on "The Novel of Slave Unrest."

Sadler established one of the first microcomputer laboratories in the United States devoted to writing, is a pioneer in computer-assisted composition (her coinage to oppose computer-assisted instruction), has coauthored software (*Diagrammatic Writing Using Word Processing*), and founded and edits the *Computer-Assisted Composition Journal,* as well as *Small College Creativity.* She is the editor of the Methodist College Press and the managing editor of the journal, *MicroPsych Network.*

Preface

With the exception of *Hotel du Lac* and *The Misalliance,* Anita Brookner's seven novels require doggedness on the part of the reader, not because they are not well written (and *very* well written) but because they are purveyors of their heroine's discomfiture and of a most discomfiting kind of discomfiture at that. The questions that come to my mind are these: If the most intelligent and most educated women so persistently muck up their personal lives and precisely in areas in which their professional expertise could guide them, then to what end intelligence and education? How can such intelligent women so consistently view the world in either-or terms, with virtually no recognition of life, stance, or choice in the middle of abundant human continua? How can the Brookner world run to such character typing?

Not that Brookner has to write about good marriages or successful women, but surely we are long since past the time when a woman's getting a doctorate and being a don automatically exclude her from participating in some of life's other felicities. Surely we are . . . ? The Brookner world remains devastatingly bleak.

Still, I relish Brookner's tightly controlled, beautifully delineated focus on human behavior, principally that of intelligent women who retain strong elements of romanticism in their makeups and approaches to life. Although this author is primarily a portrait painter of the individual heroine, known for her novels of character, she also conveys a contemporary English milieu (with strangely foreign overtones) that, because of the nature of those on whom she focuses, becomes almost a period piece. Her protagonists are generally alone but not spinsterish. Ruth Weiss in *The Debut* makes a marriage of convenience at the behest of her ailing father and is quickly widowed; at the behest of her mother, Mimi Dorn submits to a similar union with a man old enough to be her father in *Family and Friends* and loses her child but is happy in an unknowing way. Edith Hope refuses two marriages of convenience in *Hotel du Lac* to remain in thrall to her married lover; she seems to have surprised Brookner more than she has surprised the readers. Love affairs gone not simply bad but degrading have left Frances Linton of *Look at Me* and Rachel Kennedy of *A Friend from England* permanently scarred, though they react in different ways. We begin to suspect that they are driven more by neurosis than character. Kitty Maule of *Providence* misses out on the one man for her and will remain alone. *The Misalliance*'s Blanche Vernon, the divorced woman in the Brookner canon, seems to make the most headway toward recognizing her individuality and making a life for herself; then, with that full club of irony Brookner wields so persistently and so routinely—this time, we are likely to feel, on us—Blanche gets her man back.

Frequently dons or writers, the Brookner women have independent means and operate, to their detriment, from a high sense of honor and of the proper behavior for a woman. Parents, especially mothers, have usually negatively influenced these protagonists. To develop them, Brookner often adopts the techniques of foil characters and continua of female (and, increasingly, male) types—though types by and large peculiar to Brookner's world and by and large lifted, as I have decried their being lifted, from the ends of the continua only. For example, we may be presented with a "golden" person or pair to whom the heroine is attracted; with domestics who exert too much control on the family or the protagonist; with women who suffer all fools gladly and epitomize the good wife or the good neighbor; and with women who make their way with tantrums and manipulation. In a departure from the standard application, the heroine may not want to be like any of those on the continuum, though recognizing the goodness of the one extreme. In *Providence,* Kitty Maule feels that both (stupid) Caroline and (intelligent) Pauline are victimized by providence. Ironically, despite the panoply of characters set forth for their consideration, Brookner's heroines often fail to add up the many resources they can claim as unique individuals. I have wanted to shake some of them into thinking better of themselves and accepting, in some of Brookner's favorite terms, that they are "valid" and "plausible." I began to relax over my reading of her when she started letting a bit of humor slip in, mixing her language levels, and taking some swipes at the holier-than-thou. I began to applaud when a few men were allowed to speak, think, and have problems that emerge as human and not just woman centered. Alfred Dorn of *Family and Friends* is one of the best examples among all of the characters of the dimensions of the Brookner world; next to Blanche Vernon of *The Misalliance* (who will not get to use her coping strategy), he has fashioned a method of compromise, though a cynical one, that Brookner's women would do well to notice.

The world of Dr. Brookner is, partly at least, old-fashioned and lineaged. She is a descendant of Henry James and Edith Wharton, among others, with (darkened) overtones of Barbara Pym and Margaret Drabble. Readers must be literate and must, for full appreciation of her allusiveness, have some acquaintance with the legacy of the great British, Russian, and French novels and know some French. She believes, with Milton, that all of us face choices minute by minute and moral choices at least hour by hour.

A lack of resolution plays through the Brookner novels, and it may well originate in her own admiration for the French tradition, especially the works of Honoré de Balzac and Gustave Flaubert, both of whom tried to record life, to document, and to be objective, leaving readers to infer motive and extract meaning. One reason for the reliance on types may be Brookner's lineage from the sense of literature as *étude* in Balzac and his determination to throw up for assessment *la comédie humaine.* Similarly Brookner's persistent depiction of a bourgeois world against which many react, as in *Family and Friends* and *A Friend from England,* may be influenced by the types that inhabit it in Flaubert.

Whatever the reasons for the existence of this reticence—and it is surely bound up with Brookner's own drive for privacy (though she is autobiographical sometimes to excess and even uses red hair like her own in almost every book)—it is a dominant effect in the novels. They delineate details, at least surface details, and yet eschew definitiveness. In fact, the best commentary on Brookner's work may well occur in *A Friend from England* when Rachel describes the one picture that she really wants to see in the Accademia in Venice, one that combines motherhood and a mysterious male figure, the knight. While the face of the Madonna is "immanent with meaning," "all explanation" is "withdrawn." Such is Brookner's world generally, and almost no one in it reachieves that explanation, while almost no one doubts that meaning is present if it could only be found. Moreover, her dons see that meaning and fulfillment are somehow bound up with the uneasy tension among marriage, children, and the mystery of the male.

Brookner is not just writing after literary tradition, however (though she seems to make conscious comparison between her fiction and that of her nineteenth-century forebears). Here are as devastatingly critical miniature portraits as we could expect to see of the recent changes wrought in womandom (notably in Rachel's descriptions of her friends and acquaintances in *A Friend from England*) and as trenchant a portrayal of old age as can be found.

Not much happens in these novels in the modern sense—their plot is skimpy—but an inordinate amount takes place in the world of nuance; hence Brookner's Jamesianism. Sex occurs offstage but exacts an enormous toll, for example, on Frances Linton of *Look at Me* and Rachel Kennedy of *A Friend from England;* sex missed is equally consuming, as in Mimi of *Family and Friends.* At the same time, we are given strong hints of the sexual overtones in the relations of fathers and daughters and of mothers and sons. Indeed we generally sense a bit of Freud lurking about.

Brookner is not light reading. She wields an awful irony—to the point that we sometimes believe her heroines doomed from her own hand, if not from the deterministic universe she claims to eschew. She is likely, as well, to leave their sensibilities in abeyance while she makes observations that seem her own. (For a don, she also has a strange sense of commas or of the lack thereof.) Such quibbles notwithstanding, Anita Brookner is an important writer (even if my view of women—or of men—is not so jaundiced as hers).

In the pages that follow, I have tried to analyze the text closely and to let the reader do so with me. By her own admission, Brookner writes quickly, without looking back at any of the work in progress except the last chapter. The inconsistency that is occasionally to be found in the novels may well result from this strategy of composition rather than from the natural inconsistencies of life as she reflects it. Still, I hope that all of her readers will recognize, with me, how well she presents a world, if not necessarily their world, most of the time.

I wish to express my appreciation to the following publishers for permission to use and quote from the novels of Anita Brookner: to the Linden Press, of Simon & Schuster, for *The Debut* and to Pantheon Books, a division of Random House, Inc., for *Providence, Look at Me, Hotel du Lac, Family and Friends, The Misalliance,* and *A Friend from England.*

Lynn Veach Sadler

Methodist College

Chronology

Chapter One

Anita Brookner: Art Historian, Don, and Novelist

Unlike the novelist Margaret Drabble, her contemporary who has given many interviews and been very forthcoming about herself, Anita Brookner is withholding biographical information and material against a future use of her own.[1] We know broad outlines only: that she considers her family peculiar, that it has exerted a strong influence on her, that she does not judge her life to have been happy and suffers from profound loneliness even now, and that she has had two unsuccessful love affairs.[2] We might be able to pass off the indefiniteness of the novels as a way of satirizing the self-centeredness of the heroines until we come to *Family and Friends,* which is about the presumably Jewish Dorns who have fled (Eastern or Central?) Europe. World War II takes place during the time the novel describes but is not mentioned. On the other hand, the furnishings of the homes of the Dorns are lavishly (and satirically) detailed. The contrast with Drabble, who sees "every writer's work" as "a record both of himself and of the age in which he lives, as well as of the particular places he describes"[3] and whom we must read to know what London and England are like,[4] is again striking. Brookner and most of her protagonists feel that they are foreigners in their own country. We have the distinct impression that, on a personal level, they long to be like the Mousies of the world, described in *The Misalliance,* and know very well that their lives would be easier—and happier—for being so, but they simply lack the power of accommodation that comes so easily to those others:

Metaphorically, Mousie had been holding out her arms, in the certainty of meeting a welcoming embrace, since she was a little girl. . . . By holding out her baby arms Mousie had emitted the correct signals: People knew what their response should be. And because she was so delightfully forthcoming, because she was so easy to understand, because she was so artlessly pleased with the response she invariably elicited, she was allowed to be equally artless when the response was perhaps a little lacking in fervour.[5]

Thereby hangs the tale of most of Brookner's women and, in the last novels, of her men as well. They are not and never will be the Mousies of the world. The problem is that, as a result of their belaboring the contrast with themselves, they fail to recognize their own very considerable worth.

Background and Family Influence

Anita Brookner was born 16 July 1928 in London, the only child of Newson and Maude Brookner (originally Bruckner), whose origins are Polish-Jewish. Her mother gave up her career as a concert singer when she married and showed an inclination toward melancholy as a result. Her husband became angry when she tried to sing at home because only while singing did she display any passion. On such occasions, their daughter, upset by the situation, had to be carried from the room by the nanny. Anita Brookner thinks that her mother "should have been the liberated woman" in the family.[6]

Brookner grew up in an extended family. She and her parents lived with her grandmother, and there were "uncles and aunts and cousins all around" (as in the Dorns of *Family and Friends* and the Livingstones of *A Friend from England*). We have the impression that she comes closest to depicting her family grouping in *Family and Friends* and that she herself may well be the mysterious, occasionally obtrusive, narrator in that novel. This background or a similar foreign one, however, seems to penetrate many of her books (such as *The Debut* and *Providence*) and helps to account for the perception that her heroines "have a 'displaced person' quality."[7] Brookner agrees that this aspect of her characters may arise from her own feelings: "Although I was born and raised here [in London] I have never been at home, completely. People say that I am always serious and depressing, but it seems to me that the English are *never* serious—they are flippant, complacent, ineffable, but never serious, which is sometimes maddening."[8]

In any case, Brookner's family relations have certainly influenced the novels, and autobiography as a topic is visited infrequently but tellingly in several of them. Asked about the proportion of ironic detachment and identification between herself and her heroines, she responded:

I should say . . . there is a high degree of identification. This means there is also a high degree of risk. But there has to be, hasn't there, if the feeling is to come through? . . . I think it is important for the writer to take chances. . . .

To write with a very high degree of detachment . . . it doesn't seem to me that one is playing straight.[9]

Very much like Dr. Ruth Weiss in *The Debut,* for example, Brookner "was brought up to look after [her] parents." The Bruckners "were transplanted and fragile people, an unhappy brood, and [she] felt that [she] had to protect them. Indeed that is what they expected."[10] The result is many references in the novels to the heroine's growing up too quickly and yet remaining a child (e.g., *The Debut*), tortuous relations between mothers and daughters in particular (e.g., *The Misalliance*), and escape through study abroad.

Education

Brookner was educated at James Allen's Girls' School, at King's College of the University of London, where she studied French literature, and at the Courtauld Institute of Art. She has a doctorate in art history. A visiting lecturer at the University of Reading, 1959–64, she has been a reader in the history of art and has lectured at the Courtauld since 1964; she holds the rank of professor of art history. In 1967–68, she became the first woman to occupy the position of Slade Professor at the University of Cambridge and was a fellow of New Hall, Cambridge. She is also a fellow of the Royal Society of Literature. She was planning to retire from teaching when she was interviewed by Shusha Guppy for the *Paris Review* (an interview published in 1987) and will devote her time to writing more fiction and criticism. Her reason, however, is not related to the fact that she has reached the point of being able to support herself by her fiction: "I have loved teaching, and I've loved my students. Indeed I'm having the happiest year of my teaching life— perhaps because it is the last! It is just that I have taught for twenty-five years and the thought of having to go through the syllabus for the twenty-sixth year was more than I could take."[11]

Brookner's specialties are eighteenth- and nineteenth-century French art, but she is an admirer of literature too, and both interests have influenced her novels, the first of which was published when she was in her early fifties. In *The Misalliance,* Blanche Vernon is fixated on the nymphs of the National Gallery and the kouroi of the British Museum. *The Debut,* on the other hand, focuses at length on Balzac's *Eugénie Grandet; Providence,* on Benjamin Constant's *Adolphe. The Genius of the Future: Studies in French Art Criticism* is in some sense a hybridization of

her dual interests, for it examines the relations among literary figures
(Diderot, Stendhal, Baudelaire, Zola, the Brothers Goncourt, and
Huysmans) and art. The bonding between art and literature has been
constant for her:

Throughout the early 1960s and the early 70s I repaired daily to the Bibliothèque Nationale. My thoughts and hopes were entirely latent as I devoted my
main energies to reading my way laterally and diagonally through the eighteenth century. The chasms of time spent waiting for books to arrive from the
stacks encouraged browsing in the catalogue; in this way cross-references were
pursued and further request slips deposited in the boxes. The fact that these
further requests would, in their turn, take a very long time to arrive, meant
that one had to store up books to guard against rapture of the deep: the
moment when the supply would be cut off and one would sit at one's place in
the Nationale with the choice of either doing nothing or writing one's book.
Thus one would be pushed over the edge into authorship. Far better to read
the entire works of Mme de Genlis or to compile an anthology of maxims from
Duclos to Joubert. I remember taking copious notes which I lost almost
immediately afterwards. I was also becoming aware that this extraordinary way
of life was both hypnotic and fraught with danger. [12]

Brookner is a very attractive woman, [13] and the devotion of such hours
to research may help account for her remaining unmarried. An episode
in the Bibliothèque Nationale appears to be the seed for Kitty Maule
and Professor Duplessis in *Providence,* and the surprised and admiring
reaction of the library official suggests that such a setting is not fraught
with opportunities to develop the famous viability endlessly sought by
Brookner's heroines.

To anyone seeking a distraction from mere reading there was little to hand. I
had long ago given up glancing hopefully at my neighbours, most of whom
seemed to be narrow-faced men of a certain age and a suspicious cast of feature;
I imagined that they were all working on the Dreyfus case and trying to reverse
the verdict. One sensational day a man whom I knew slightly burst through
the various *cordons sanitaires*—without reader's ticket! without laissez-passer!
without briefcase!—to place a bunch of roses on my desk, and when I left that
evening, the customs officer at the main desk slowly removed his peaked cap,
equally slowly persuaded his features to relax into a smile, and then said, in an
excruciatingly loud voice, "Bonne chance, Mademoiselle." Otherwise, nothing
happened. [14]

Brookner finds differences but a greater similarity between writing criticism and writing fiction: "In fiction you give too much away while in criticism you can hide behind another writer's personality and work. For me both are ways of working through a problem. I liken the whole process to writing an examination paper—you have a certain amount of time and space and you have to do your best. It is nerve-racking but not particularly difficult."[15] Still, she will not write on art history again: "That particular career is over. Once you have let it go you can't go back. I shall not give up studying, but I might do it with words rather than pictures, although pictures will come into it."[16]

We expect Brookner to be well read, but the range she has covered is unusual even for a don who combines expertise in art history and an interest in literature.[17] She read French literature while studying French in college and admits to being influenced by Balzac, Stendhal, and Flaubert, and particularly by the second, as well as by Proust. Zola was her favorite when she was younger; although she disagrees with his determinism, she pairs him with Dickens for "courage," "indignation," and anger "at the unfairness of things."[18] She has read the great German writers, too (including Kleist and Goethe), and took up the subject of romanticism after hearing Isaiah Berlin trace the problems of the modern age back to romanticism and the Germans. A quotation from Goethe's *Sorrows of Young Werther* provides the epigraph for *Family and Friends*. Among the English, she cites Trollope "for decent feelings" and George Eliot "for moral seriousness." "Of course," she says, she has read "the great Russians." She is willing to trace the moral grounding of her characters to two sources: the nineteenth-century novel and the moral strictness of her family. In fact, all of the concern of her characters to be valid and her own wish to be "more plausible, flattering, frivolous" trace to these same sources. American influences are Henry James (who "has all the moral conscience that everybody should have") and Edith Wharton (in whose "great novels the moral option is nearly always taken by the women"), the two she most wishes to resemble. Of contemporary literature, she reads "everything that comes out" and even buys the hardbacks to support her fellow writers. At the time of the interview with Guppy, she was rereading Philip Roth, whom she "adores." Others cited are Rosamond Lehmann (to whom she dedicates *Hotel du Lac*), Elizabeth Taylor, Storm Jameson, Ivy Compton-Burnett, and Jean Rhys in the English tradition; the Czech Edith Templeton; and Canadians Mavis Gallant and Edith de Born. She singles out Peter Ackroyd and Yann Quéffelec as "imaginative" writers. In an earlier

telephone interview, she included Saul Bellow, Alison Lurie, and Arthur Cohen.[19] In the Guppy interview, oddly, she does not mention
either Margaret Drabble or Barbara Pym, with whom she is most often
compared.

Brookner seems to have experienced few difficulties balancing the
demands of the various facets of her professional lives. In addition to
teaching and working as an art critic at the Courtauld, she has been able
to write her fiction there, at least in the summers when the institute is
closed to the public. She writes only when she is not working, and each
novel has been written during the summer and in some three to four
months. While writing, she works all day every day but not in the
evening, when she tries "to switch off completely and not think about it
till the next day." Guppy reports that her office is filled with books and
pictures of French paintings and that her desk has an old typewriter and
is covered with papers. She also works at home in Chelsea in her small but
sunny and quiet apartment furnished in light colors and overlooking a
large, pleasant communal garden. Her adaptability is further demon-
strated by the fact that she can write "anywhere":

In my flat, or in my office at the Courtauld. I have even written on a bus.
When you live in a small flat you write on the edge of things—there is no
great set-up. I type what I have written at the office. I prefer working there
because I like the interruptions—telephone calls, visitors. I am completely
schizophrenic, as I can carry on a conversation in my head while another,
apparently sensible conversation, is taking place with someone who has just
come into the room. At home the isolation weighs on me. It is a terrible
strain.[20]

Unlike her heroines, she uses long walks to wind down after her stint of
writing is finished for the day. While she is "grateful for the life in the
streets—the people, the shopwindows,"[21] they walk literally to *kill*
time and give no evidence of being interested in what they pass as they
walk. Nonetheless, she is akin to them in considering herself "one of
the loneliest women in London. People have resented it—it is not done
to confess to loneliness, but there it is."[22]

The Brookner Canon

Anita Brookner began her writing career as a scholar of art history.
She published *Watteau* in 1967, *The Genius of the Future: Studies in French*

Art Criticism in 1971, *Greuze: The Rise and Fall of an Eighteenth Century Phenomenon* in 1972, and *Jacques-Louis David* in 1974. She continues to provide reviews and articles (e.g., on Rousseau, Mme de Staël, the Bibliothèque Nationale) for such publications as the *Times Literary Supplement*, the *Spectator*, the *Observer*, *Burlington Magazine*, the *London Review of Books*, and the London *Times*. While she is now best known for her novels, her "book on David is considered a model of the genre, combining as it does biography, history and criticism."[23]

Brookner says that her start as a writer of fiction "was literally trying [her] hand. . . . [She] wondered how it was done and the only way to find out seemed to be to try and do it." She was also going through a bad patch at the time and thought that writing what was happening to her might help to explain why she deserved such a fate.[24] The result was *A Start in Life* (1981), published in the United States as *The Debut* and an instant success with critics and the reading public. Surely she has set something of a record, for she has had a novel published each year since then: *Providence* in 1982; *Look at Me* in 1983, though it was brought out in the United States before *Providence; Hotel du Lac,* which won the Booker-McConnell Prize for Fiction and was later filmed for television (1986), in 1984; *Family and Friends,* which became a bestseller in England and the United States, in 1985; *A Misalliance (The Misalliance* in the United States), in 1986; and *A Friend from England* in 1987. In the interview with Shusha Guppy in the *Paris Review* in 1987, she reported that she was currently working on the next novel but "taking it slowly."[25] Given her rate of production, however, it is surely completed or near completion by now.

Known as a model of prose style and particularly for aptness of word choice, Brookner disclaims having a style or thinking about her words. Rather, she concentrates on what the words want to say and aims, above all, to be lucid: "You might say that lucidity is a conscious preoccupation." She never rewrites any part of a novel but the last chapter. Further, her fiction is not planned out; she has an idea but does not know what will happen; she simply lets the book take over and work itself along. She does not consider herself imaginative or inventive but "examine[s] the behavior of characters, the possibilities: why this way and not that way?" Because her works of fiction tend to be the same length and are most often slight variants of each other, she has been accused of writing to a formula, albeit one she has created. Her later novels, she believes, defy such charges.[26]

Chapter Two
A Start in Life/The Debut: "Unsafe against Disappointment"
The Novel

In *The Debut* (1981; published as *A Start in Life* in England), forty-year-old Dr. Ruth Weiss, who specializes in but fails to learn from the women of Balzac, looks back at her abortive "start in life" or "debut." As a child and now as a woman, she has been generally dismissed as meek and uninteresting, not worth speculation. She copes by remembering that, at one point in her life, she has "known great terror, great emotion" and has "been entrusted with . . . a strenuous part" in a play from life: real literature as opposed to that in books yet the kind that people cannot tolerate except on a page (10). That part is not her having been loved by a leading (and married) philologist at the Sorbonne, who is, in any case, much older and simply a nice man, but her having been recalled by family duty virtually at the onset of her breakaway life in Paris.

Ruth has grown up in a divided household. Her grandmother, for whom she is named, has escaped from a dark past in Germany (but not from its legacy) and has brought her dark furniture and darker gloom with her. Ruth's father, Georg, quick to change his name to "George," marries a woman the antithesis of his mother. Helen, who is detested by her mother-in-law, dwells only in the immediate present and only on herself (as will the much younger Sally Beamish, a minor character in *The Misalliance*). Ruth's grandmother presides over the dining room; her mother, over the drawing room, later retreating to life in the bedroom when she no longer gets the parts she wants in light stage comedies. Ruth's father, perhaps because he is male, can move fairly easily between the two worlds of these women to eat boiled eggs at the table with his mother and gourmet tidbits in bed with his wife. The child, largely ignored by her mother, lives the life of her grandmother. When Ruth's grandmother, the nurturing figure in the novel, dies, Mrs. Cutler, another widow, moves in to run the household. She is, by choice and powers of manipulation, as ineffectual as the two adults and becomes another "playmate" for them, particularly for Helen. Ruth learns to get her own meals: "spinsterish [Barbara Pym] fare" of eggs, boiled potatoes, and salads (21), a fitting preparation for her bleak future.

Ruth's only outlet is literature and school, where her ability in French earns her the interest of a teacher (Miss Parker) and ultimately entry into college. Bored and unhappy at home, she stays in the library as much as possible or walks to pass the time, a standard coping device of Brookner heroines, when the library is closed. Her boredom is finally pierced: she is congratulated by Richard Hirst for winning a British Council scholarship to complete her dissertation in France. She promptly falls in love with this first of many golden men in Brookner's novels and moves into a flat in Edith Grove in the hopes of entertaining him at dinner, an example of the overinvestment of Brookner women in romantic dreams of the "very solidly English, Protestant men" who flit through their lives, just out of reach.[2] They never seem to understand that "most men accept invitations to dinner simply in order to know where the next meal is coming from" (55). A psychologist and student counselor, Richard collects problem characters, one of whom deters his arrival at Ruth's until late on the evening of the fateful dinner, which is spoiled. To her mild remonstrance, he reacts with the (ironic) accusation that Ruth never thinks of others. She ends up lending him a hundred pounds to help the current runaway wife/mother in distress and moves back home, where she pays rent and waits to go to Paris on her scholarship.

Her father consents for Ruth to go to France only when she agrees to room with Humphrey and Rhoda Wilcox, former customers of the rare-book store George stocks with books his father managed to have sent out of Germany.[3] Eighty-year-old Humphrey, a writer of popular histories of French heroes, spies on her through a crack in the bathroom wall. Ruth's world, dreary by any standard, continues to be dreary even in Paris. She stays away from her "maid's" [probably an unintended pun] room as much as possible but has to return to bathe at a certain hour in accordance with the rules of the house. In Paris her old pattern of walking to pass the time reasserts itself. During one of her outings to the Louvre, she feels her luck changing when she sees and later meets the golden couple of this book, Hugh and Jill Dixon, and promptly begins to sleep without dreaming, a sign to her that her life has changed for the better. They take her in tow, allow her to buy them meals, and show her the way to "improve herself" with a haircut and more fashionable clothing. Her spirits lift, and she begins to think of the world in terms of "Balzacian opportunism" (110).[4] Unaffected when Hugh (a dealer in Old Master drawings who is young but has white hair) tries to make love to her, she meets Professor Duplessis in the Bibliothèque Nationale and feels that she might yet be "redeemed" by love (115).

At home, George has sold his rare-book shop to widow Sally Jacobs with whom he begins an affair that puts an end to his previous one with his assistant, Miss Moss. While he and Helen are on a vacation at Molly Edwards's cottage in Hove, Mrs. Cutler starts to think of marrying again and puts her name in at a marriage bureau. The announcement of her impending marriage to Leslie Arthur Dunlop brings on a crisis, and George, unable to cope with Helen and wanting in any case to be freer to associate with Sally, tries to call Ruth to demand that she come home and look after her mother. He thus discovers that Ruth has left the Wilcoxes.

At the time Ruth finally receives the call to duty (ironically the call to "return to her father"), she has just completed the decoration of the apartment vacated by the Dixons; has purchased wine and practiced cooking a special cake ("le Marquis") for Duplessis, a man old enough to be her father; and is ready to entertain her lover, whom she has put off until everything is just right. Again analyzing her experience in accordance with her forced interpretation of literature, she feels in control of life and no longer identifies with Balzac's Eugénie Grandet. The episode is the dinner for Richard Hirst written larger.

Already this next crisis has magnified, however. Helen overhears George saying goodnight to Sally over the telephone, realizes that he is having an affair, and drives him from the house. When Ruth returns home, Helen refuses to stay, and they make a difficult journey to Molly's. While they are away, George suffers a mild stroke at Sally's, and Mrs. Cutler has to call to bring Ruth to his hospital bed. Helen dies in the London cab on the way to their house.

Recovering enough to leave the hospital, George goes home with Ruth. Sally is at first attentive but gradually turns away and leaves London to stay with her sister. Professor Duplessis calls several times, but George, now almost deaf, dismisses him as a wrong number. Ruth becomes reconciled to her lot, gets an assistant lectureship, and writes. She is assertive enough at least on professional grounds to maintain a flat of her own until she marries Sally's nephew Roddy. The marriage takes place, however, because of her father's wishes. At any rate, she even begins to feel a sense of security for about the only time in her life, a signal to Brookner devotees that the untoward is about to be loosed. The couple moves in with George. After only six months, Ruth's husband is killed in an automobile accident. She sells the rare-book shop, spends two nights a week in the Edith Grove flat working at her writing, and permits her life to settle into her work on Balzac and her commitment to her father.

Looking to Literature

In many ways, the relation of Brookner's heroines to literature reminds us of Margaret Drabble, particularly of Rosamund Stacey in *The Millstone* (or *Thank You All Very Much*), as well as of Flaubert's Emma Bovary, who not only confuses life and literature but misreads both. Ruth blames her life on literature, even claiming that that life is more real than literature, but does not see, for example, that it has a wholeness to it that smacks of the completion that is a literary end. Structurally, the "book" that she "tells" (in a third-person voice that is remarkably first-person) begins and ends with her plaguing Ned, her publisher, to bring out the next of her volumes on Balzac (8, 192). Substantively her life as cast in this telling is literature of the type of Gustave Flaubert's "A Simple Heart" or Sherwood Anderson's "Death in the Woods" or even e. e. cummings's "[nobody loses all the time]." While none of us may wish to live the patterns of these four, all of us would like to have pattern, particularly the heightening pattern of art. The irony is that this scholar of literature is oblivious of the painful literary cut of her own tale as she is oblivious of the parallels between the lives of the heroines of French literature on whom she is an authority and her own failed life. She both believes in and relies on literature and yet refuses somehow to learn from it.

Instead Ruth distances herself from others through literature; her "debut" in life is, to her at least, highly dramatic literature (literally a "play" into one of whose roles she was thrust). No one else is aware of this personal drama because she does not recognize that she has also accepted the mold into which others have cast her and has never, from childhood and despite her intelligence, done anything to change that image. Even thoughtful, brave Molly Edwards, her mother's arthritic and Christian Science friend and a retired comedy actress, dismisses Ruth as lacking the spirit of her mother and being in the mold of her grandmother, a conventional woman (170) and one of the first characters to represent "middle-class" values in Brookner's novels. Mrs. Cutler enjoys being alone when Helen and George visit Molly; she does not count Ruth (95), though the two strike up a quite satisfactory arrangement, and Mrs. Cutler becomes, momentarily, the surrogate mother she has not had since the death of her grandmother.

Ruth both misreads literature, and consequently life, and blames literature for her life. Never having had a real mother, she has had to grow up fast to attend to the needs of her family, much as Brookner describes her own life. The result is that she, like Brookner, "became an adult too soon and paradoxically never grew up."[5] She is enabled to assume responsibility and seriousness so quickly, again like Brookner, largely by reading "sad but improving books" that have made her eager "to join this upward movement toward the light" (11), a stance also strong in the heroines of Margaret Drabble. In the works of Charles Dickens[6] and the many Everyman editions with which her father supplies her, she sees the "moral universe" unveiled but, a trait constant with her, "hardly notice[s] that her home resembled the one she was reading about: a superficial veil of amusement over a deep well of disappointment" (11). She recognizes the contradiction in the "faulty moral education" of the literature to which she has been exposed— being asked to ponder the careers of Anna Karenina[7] and Emma Bovary but to emulate those of David Copperfield and Little Dorrit (7)—but goes on acting on what she hopes is possible at the moment. During the months of her grandmother's dying, she maintains a vigil with her books to sustain her, and, when the death occurs, she simply turns back to the book she is reading, Brookner's way of symbolizing Ruth's reliance on literature. Looking back, she uses an allusion to Dickens's *A Tale of Two Cities*—"It was the best of times, it was the worst of times" (17)—to describe her childhood, though she constantly defies Dickens's morally ordered universe and is quite wrong about her entirely wretched childhood. While herself blaming Eugénie Grandet's parents for the defection of their daughter's lover, she cannot make herself break away from her own, who ignore or use her. At the end of the book, when Mrs. Cutler returns for a visit and suggests that Ruth put her father in a nursing home, she will not, for, though he has repeatedly tried to make her feel guilty at the least thought of leaving home, she remembers that he "had had style; he could not end up like this" (190). Ruth, a woman of old-fashioned and out-of-fashion virtues, is, finally, something of a self-made martyr, another literary role in which she has largely cast herself.

One of the greatest ironies of the novel, however, is the kind of literature that has most influenced the protagonist. As a child, she fell asleep over her nurse's promise that "Cinderella *shall* go to the ball" (7), and, despite her learning, her authority as a professor of literature, she still expects, in defiance of life and in defiance of the kind of literature she analyzes and teaches, that she *will* someday go to the ball. (So most Brookner heroines believe, though Rachel Kennedy in *A Friend from England* wants to set them straight.) The "innocent and hopeless love" of Balzac's Eugénie Grandet makes Ruth uncomfortable, for it flies in the face of the Cinderella story. If her nurse had only read her a translation of the Balzac, with its plaintive but truthful, "Je ne suis pas assez belle pour lui" ("I am not beautiful enough for him"), Ruth feels that her whole life might have been different. She does not see that the nurse in *Eugénie Grandet* tried to build some character into her charge (154) and that being "so listless, so absent, so unhappy" (154) can be controlled by the individual. Neither Eugénie nor Ruth changes. As it is, no matter what Balzac or other writers tell this heroine and despite the play on "wise" in her last name, she keeps hoping for the ball. She knows that Balzac teaches the irrelevance of moral fortitude and the "supreme effectiveness of bad behavior" (36), a constant contrast observed by Brookner's women (who nonetheless stay in the former category), but consoles herself with her own lack of manipulative powers, "which distinguished the villains [of Balzac] from the virtuous" (49), while wishing that her life was different. She had rather be, for all that, a "bad winner than a good loser" (150). Yet she does "not understand, and few women do, that Balzac's rascally heroes are in fact consumed with a sense of vocation, in which love plays only an evanescent if passionate part, that they will go on and on and on and never rest until death cuts them down" (154). Hugh, the second golden man to whom she is exposed, in an aside to himself bears out Balzac's view of men and of love: "Hugh looked at her [Ruth] and thought of his beautiful wife, of whom he had such doubts. Ruth, in so many and such surprising ways the better woman, would never measure up, he thought. In that moment he threw in his lot with Jill and the baby she would have. He could not do without her. But he smiled kindly at Ruth, grateful to her for making up his mind" (148).

Similarly, Dr. Ruth Weiss draws her knowledge of love principally from literature and yet hopes to fly in the face of what she gleans of it there. When she follows her friend Anthea's advice about making herself more attractive and wins the scholarship to France, the only change that matters to her is falling, as she supposes, in love with Richard on the simple basis that he congratulated her and took her to lunch. She sees, through Balzac's Eugénie, that she is not attractive enough for Richard but falls in love anyway, to the chagrin of worldly Anthea (one of the foils for her in the novel), who knows that "Richard is a prize beyond the expectations of most women, and certainly those of Ruth" (40–41), who is "attractive enough for a clever woman, but it was only as a clever woman that she was attractive" (40). Ruth is never able, however, to take "literary" comfort from the "hopeless passion" with which she could imbue her case. Much later, when she receives a letter from Richard returning her loan and saying that he is getting married, she reacts with tears and depression, though he has done nothing to feed her hopes as Maurice feeds Kitty's in *Providence*. Ruth remains trapped between waiting for the ball as possible and knowing that she is too unattractive to be invited. The truth is in between— territory that the Brookner women never, to their loss, seem to explore and have acquaintance with. Ruth has as much right to the ball as any other woman but has to work for it. We readers may become impatient with her for not shaking loose her beautiful red hair (another memory of the author in this very autobiographical book)[8] and appropriating some of the confidence of her red-haired mother.

An expert in literature, Ruth frequently lets it drive rather than reflect life. Thus, based on her reading, she thinks that she knows how most women in love fill the day (49) but is wrong, according to Brookner, about what love is like (83). With so many of the other Brookner heroines, she takes one small episode (Richard's kindness) and expands it to romantic passion written large. On the other hand, Ruth is blind to the one man in the book who is, though married, nonetheless suitable as her lover. When Hugh tries to make love to her, she is amazed and wants to know why (110). Duplessis, the father figure, in contrast, becomes her ideal lover, though he too is married (and happily). If she instinctively knows that he is "not her ideal or a romantic lover," she does not seem aware that romantic love grows with the lover's absence (115). Both he and Hugh fit the figure of her dream, "a person of indeterminate sex with gray hair" who leaves her when her enormous hunger[9] prevents her from entertaining that companion. In fact, were it not for her romantic preconceptions of love, gleaned principally from literature or from other women who have imbibed the romantic view of love in literature, she would be quite content with her intellectual lot. Brookner tells us that Ruth approaches her essays "as many women approach a meeting with a potential lover" (32).

An unusual feature in *The Debut* is that the minor figures are not only character foils for the protagonist but foils for her misappropriation of and contradictory approach to literature. Helen, whose name suggests a literary counterpart (as Ruth's suggests a biblical one), imagines that she has had a risqué life, the stuff of racy autobiography. When she can no longer find work, she stays in bed and plays at writing the lurid details. While she has had affairs, one of them with the husband of her friend Molly, she imagines that George has been faithful to her and is undone and distraught when she finds out the truth of the case. Molly, slowly dying, recognizes the deterioration of her friend but sees that Helen will be "taken unawares" (92), as her daughter, Ruth, is in ordinary episodes again and again in the novel. Ironically, however, Helen becomes addicted to "literature" that depicts a life opposite to that she has led. Living her life out in bed, she reads a novel a day, preferably one she has read before. The books are identical: nineteenth-century maidens become governesses and lose their hearts to the rakish son, though they never consummate their love. Helen thinks that the mistake of her life may have been the consummation.

Literature is important to many in the novel and is often misused. Helen gives one of Molly's Christian Science books, for entirely inappropriate reasons, to Mrs. Cutler. She has heretofore kept it at her bedside with several novels by Georgette Heyer. Molly herself reads Henry James, as we have seen, one of the writers especially admired by Anita Brookner. George, who is a poor businessman and is able to earn a living only because of his father's cache of rare books, has no appreciation for literature himself but has fed Ruth's love of it. His former mistress is also a great reader.

Foil Characters and Character Types

The use of foil characters is a technique that becomes common in Brookner's novels and may well derive most immediately from Flaubert and particularly Balzac. She calls attention to it in this book, her own debut as a fiction writer: Ruth's friend Anthea, like Helen, needs a foil (as well as an acolyte [33]), and Ruth and George are foils for Helen and

Anthea (36). The literary characters dissected by Ruth, especially Balzac's Eugénie Grandet and her nurse, are also foils. The principal foil
characters, however, are those around her: her own mother, who does
know how to use her red hair to advantage; Molly Edwards, her
mother's friend, who as a Christian Scientist displays a different kind of
renunciation; Anthea, Ruth's own "beautiful friend," who, with the
overt physical appeal that Ruth hides and denies in herself, yet is
insecure and must play sexual games; Sally Jacobs, who has an affair
with Ruth's father not so much to have a sexual affair as to have a man
to feed again, while George, considered by others in the novel as
cutting something of a grand figure and fitting the role of the man
about town, is interested in Sally primarily because of the comfort her
flat affords him; and the Dixons, the golden pair, who live largely off
others, while the great beauty of Jill seems merely to make her promis-
cuous and to keep her from wanting what other women value (for
example, children). Also present is the overbearing domestic, Mrs.
Cutler, who, having turned up her nose at Helen for still being interested in sex, decides to get married again for companionship and status
and thus mirrors to some extent what happens to Ruth with Roddy.
Even the slight portraits of Miss Howe and Miss Mackendrick, who
have flats in Edith Grove, give Ruth a glimpse of the Barbara Pym
world of the spinster, in this case the "fierce and argumentative" and
the "sweet and vague," respectively. We are likely to be left with the
overwhelming sense, however, that whether the case is a character in
literature or in her life, Ruth, for all her introspection, never applies
the lessons set before her. She remains a kind of female version of John
Marcher in Henry James's "The Beast in the Jungle," a willing victim
of passivity.

The Novel as Novel

The Debut not only establishes a Brookner technique (reliance on foil
characters) but an approach to character of a certain hue. The heroines
of these novels, like those of the works of Barbara Pym, live life at a
reduced level. They also have more than a glint of autobiographical
revelation (for example, the Weisses living with Ruth's grandmother):

Raised in an eccentric Polish family in London, Brookner felt the limitations
of her environment at an early age. The opportunity to study offered, among
other things, the chance to escape her family and to explore new territory by

traveling to France. Becoming a scholar, however, kept Brookner in academia for most of her life and never offered her the conventions of family and marriage. Despite her successful career, there remains an element of regret in the author's view of her own life. "I wanted to get married," she confessed in an interview. "As it is, I've never really left school. That's my sad story." Her fictional explorations of romantic myths reflect this disillusionment: her books are written in a sorrowful tone[,] and her heroines display a kind of melancholy acceptance of their inability to alter their situations.[10]

Brookner escapes to France for art; Ruth Weiss, for literature, specifically Balzac, though Brookner herself is a devotee of French literature. Brookner's Polish family becomes in this first novel Ruth's German grandmother, whose entire heritage is at odds with the lightweight insouciance of her daughter-in-law Helen, an aging, childlike actress of drawing-room comedies. George changes his first name as Newson Bruckner changed the family name ("Like calling yourself Batethoven!").[11] For all of the similarities, however, Brookner has apparently come to terms with her life—and its success—while her heroines, at most, accept their diminished lot. Even when Ruth, for example, contrasts her students and herself, finding them "bolder," "large, clear-eyed, and beautiful," with voices "ringing with confidence," though their translations are "narrow and cautious" (8), she is unable to conclude that her academic prowess is worth as much, much less more. She and other Brookner heroines seem unable to value rightly what they do have. Trying to cheer up Hugh at the thought that Jill's baby may not be his ("There's usually another man around. She's always been the same. So beautiful, you see" [147]), she admits, "with difficulty," "not everybody is allowed to have a baby" (147). Brookner may also justify her use of autobiography in *The Debut,* for she allows Ruth to "understand" "Balzac's sense of cosmic energy, in which all the characters are submerged until thrown up again like atoms, to dance on the surface of one particular story, to disappear, to reappear in another guise, in another novel" (154–55).

More tightly constructed and more ironic and depressing than most other first novels and centered on the depiction of Ruth's character, *The Debut* is yet marked by a tendency to deposit analysis and then move on to the plot. As if conscious of the differences in these two kinds of material and approach and of their competition, Brookner adopts the reminiscential narrator (Ruth) to carry the weight of the substantive portion of the novel and makes Ruth's tale third-person. Still, the reader is likely to feel that the bridgework is not entirely successful. Brookner is forced to intrude with authorial comment to tell us what we are to think. As examples, Ruth is said to know, "without understanding, that Mrs. Cutler [i]s one of those louche [a recurrent term in Brookner] women who thrive on the intimacy of couples" (21), and Anthea has "already run through the entire gamut of adult female experience, from promiscuity to dyed blond streaks in the hair" (35).

On the other hand, we can accept that this narrative "flaw" is meant to call attention to the contradictions and conflicts that lace the life and character of Ruth and, seemingly, in Brookner, of life in general. The first such contradiction is in the startling (and very effective) opening: "Dr. Weiss, at forty, knew that her life had been ruined by literature" (7). In short order, we learn that, as an authority on the women of Balzac, she makes her living by literature. Nonetheless, she blames her old-fashioned looks on literature (8) and her style of dress (pleated skirts, cardigans, and saddle shoes) on the teachers of literature she has emulated. Her beautiful long red hair, a feature whose counterpart she can find in literature (and in her creator) and her one "undisciplined attribute," she hides/tames in a "classical" chignon (8); it has also made her head ache when she was a child (11). Similarly, she appears virginal but only from the effects of an attack of meningitis (8),[12] and both her appearance and her character are "exactly halfway between the nineteenth and twentieth centuries" (8). Scrupulous and passionate, she is a contradiction in personality, though others consider her merely the former while she is in fact "extreme in everything" (8). She prefers men but is an authority on women (8), at least on those of Balzac, though she never seems capable of avoiding their mistakes in her own life.[13] Such contradictions cleverly underscore the great conflict of the novel: Ruth's loving her parents while knowing full well that they are "unsafe against disappointment" (16), as is everything in her life but her work. Interestingly, the novel explores the nexus of self-protection and responsibility to others, but Ruth is never able to gauge her case in such terms. What happens to her happens largely because she lets it happen. She does not have such ill luck with men because, as Helen thinks, they are put off by women who are bluestockings (27). Nor is her case a simple one of being among the unlucky rather than the lucky, as it might well be if she were the creation of Margaret Drabble. Ruth just fails to self-assess and move on. Her lot is being "thrust into" and "cast" for roles not of her own volition. The portrait Brookner paints of Ruth is careful and exact. That it is not fetching may be the result of its exactness (though the other portrait drawn at great length, despite its depiction of Helen's deliquescence, is both exact and appealing).[14] More than likely, however, we readers simply want to shake some good common sense into this heroine and tell her to use those brains and get on with her life. Her plight derives principally from character rather than neurosis, however. She does not, like Madame Bovary, kill herself; she does not, like Eugénie Grandet, immolate herself by giving her life to works of charity. The work into which she escapes is useful, nonetheless, and the Balzac she dissects may issue in richer effects for others who construe its messages differently.

Chapter Three
Providence: "No Middle Way"
The Legacy of Literature Again

In Brookner's second novel, *Providence* (1982), perhaps her most ironic and another with autobiographical overlays, Kitty Maule specializes in the romantic tradition, one of Brookner's own areas of expertise, and wins an appointment as a teacher in a provincial university.[1] Her creator, of course, teaches at the Courtauld Institute. Kitty's Russian, French, and English background, which ought to make her appealingly romantic and exotic, instead seems to convey her to others as strange and remote and reminds the reader of Brookner's eccentric Polish family and of Ruth Weiss's German extraction in *The Debut*. Her "family history" is "perhaps a little colourful" (5), we are told. Neither English nor French, she feels that she belongs nowhere. Her grandfather Vadim is Russian, and, when he met her grandmother, he was a member of an acrobat act. Maman Louise was a French seamstress, who moved to London to make her fortune and eventually had a salon on Grosvenor Street, which she ran with Vadim's help until she had a heart attack. Their granddaughter, born Catherine Joséphine Thérèse, is "Thérèse" at home with her grandparents and "Kitty" everywhere else. Because she disappears on weekends, when she visits them in the suburbs, people think that she must live in the country; because her grandmother dresses her so well, her friends think that she must be from the city.

Even more than usual in the Brookner canon, the protagonist feels distanced from others, forced always to try to fit in but knowing that she does not. Her fashionable clothes and money also keep her from being assimilated. Like other Brookner heroines, then, she is well off materially but is not her own person. She persistently allows her life to be shaped by others and by circumstance. Her stylishness is not of her choosing and in fact rather embarrasses her, for it is quite out of keeping, she feels, with the university environment. Again like Ruth Weiss, Kitty is beset by contradictions, as are Brookner women in general.

Kitty believes that she has received little from her mother, a quiet, ineffectual, frail figure with anemia and a heart murmur, who was turned into a kind of pampered guest by her parents. Marie-Thérèse married Captain John Maule after he accompanied his sister to Louise's shop where she was acting as hostess. He left for the front immediately after their honeymoon and was killed in action. Kitty's mother died quietly sitting at the table with walnut shells in her hand. Afterward, her daughter has difficulty eating except the meals she prepares for her occasional lover, Maurice Bishop, with whom her brief affair, against Kitty's wishes, has turned into a strange kind of friendship, a "comradely routine" (19).

An unbeliever in things spiritual, Kitty nonetheless has a strong superstitious bent (100).[2] At her neighbor Caroline's suggestion, she goes to visit Madame Eva (alias Mrs. Cartwright) to have her fortune read, and on her second visit learns that she herself is a little psychic. She is "intellectually, as well as morally, uneasy" (64) about this approach, and her shame throws into relief more forcefully her blindness about love, a blindness that denigrates the lessons of the literature she knows and teaches so well. As readers, we may well feel uneasy viewing the trained analytic mind operating at the personal level on a "clutching-at-straws" basis. We feel the irony in Kitty's being energized by what she learns from Madame Eva; she knows that she must act to claim the advantage hinted at by the seer, so she calls Maurice, says that she too is going to France, and asks if they can meet. We want her to become assertive but for the right reason: to reclaim herself, not to get Maurice, who is not worth having.

As is customary in Brookner, then, the heroine is in love with the wrong man. An expert on romanticism, she is unaware of falling prey to and being intrigued by Maurice's "romantic" blending of interests in history and cathedrals and by the tale of the fiancée who renounced him to work with Mother Teresa. Similarly, Ruth Weiss in *The Debut* never managed to absorb the lessons of the French literature that was her specialty. At the end, when she attends a dinner party he is giving in her honor, she learns that he will marry one of her students, a member of his own social class and a family neighbor. Kitty, now thirty, will spend the rest of her life alone. Her only other lover has been Jean-Claude, her grandmother Louise's great-nephew, and he is now married.

We are likely to have the impression that Brookner is consciously reacting to her own portrait of passive acceptance in *The Debut*. This heroine leads and will lead the same diminished existence as Ruth Weiss but is at least able to articulate a view of life that is more assertive and more positive: "For everyone turns into something else, and I can do it too" (159). Knowing that she is not old enough for the staid and orderly way of life she has come to lead (49) and obeying, like her Brookner sisters, "sedulously careful rituals for outwitting the long nights" (36), Kitty looks straight at the future and knows that she can live it: "a life of very great fullness and happiness, teaching, learning, taking notes, taking note; she saw herself calm, and pleasant, and controlled, and suitable" (160), though she later that same night "burned in fires" thinking of Maurice. Nonetheless, we fear that the very roteness of this recitation, like the automatic recital of her family background she has come to throw up for questioners, will result in artificiality. Indeed her own inability to trust the words of others drives her to impose this image of her orderly world in the first place and sends her to repeating, as if counting off the beads of a rosary or fashioning a world after that of Balzac's Eugénie Grandet, "her life's work of establishing the true and the good and perhaps the beautiful, of believing the best of everyone, of enjoying what life offered, not lamenting what it withheld" (6). Equally artificial is the source of this credo, which she believes "was how her father had been" (6). In reality, she knows nothing about her father, who died before she was born, but she keeps his picture in her flat as a virtual shrine. He, like Maurice Bishop, represents the pure "Englishness" that could solve her feeling of rootlessness, and the two are linked by her: "She had made the young soldier in the faded photograph her image of England just as she had made Maurice her ideal of England" (159). Like Ruth Weiss, she is as driven by her father as if she interacted with him daily.[3] She is also as self-deceived as Ruth. Vadim and Louise, her grandparents, of whom she is faintly ashamed, are the real source of her resilient attitude toward life: their home is filled with sadness (because of the tragic life of their daughter, Marie-Thérèse) but never with despair or depression (6).

The Legacy of Literature

Standardly in Brookner, as in her contemporary Margaret Drabble, the heroines are nurtured by literature and by the romanticized legacy of the pseudo-literary folk tradition, particularly as the latter has to do with the lore of women. Kitty is highly susceptible to both and ironically so because she is simultaneously a romantic or "romanticist" (by profession) and no romantic (when she eschews that found romantic by others). She idolizes the image of the young soldier-father, kissing his bride goodbye and dying bravely in action, but misses the romantic image of her physically and spiritually damaged mother, quietly waiting for the young soldier who is never to return. She is in fact oblivious to all of the legacies of her mother but particularly of Marie-Thérèse's addiction to romantic novels, despite the fact that Kitty herself often borrowed these to read in place of, ironically, what she should have been reading, the books on her subject, the romantic tradition. Kitty is another female don whose specialty makes her submission to romanticizing and to selective romanticizing even more ironic than Ruth's in *The Debut*. An excellent teacher and lecturer—her lecture on the romantic tradition wins her a full-time post at the university—she is nonetheless as victimized by romanticism as her mother is by its bastardized form in the romantic novels that pass time for her.

Maurice Bishop is the essence of the romantic figure and is even attracted to the romanticism of his own woeful tale, but he is finally a romantic poseur, and Kitty misses the artifice. While constantly exchanging endearments with her, he withholds details, we surmise, to cultivate his own mysteriousness. In his defense, however, he cannot know, except as another professional might know, Kitty's belief in the message of the way words are handled. She tells her students as they study Benjamin Constant's *Adolphe:* "A novel is not simply a confession, you know. It is about the author's choice of words. . . . I am sorry to hammer this point but you must take notice of how the words are handled, in which context they are used. They will tell you everything" (45).[4] Maurice cannot, of course, know how much weight Kitty will give his words. She at first hears rumors and ultimately solicits his story. Two months before their wedding, his childhood sweetheart Lucy renounced the world and went off to work with Mother Teresa in India. When Maurice recites the tale to Kitty, he embroiders it richly but leaves out one fact that he is unlikely not to know already: that he will replace Lucy with another golden girl who will complement him (and reproduce the golden pair of *The Debut* and of the upcoming *Look at Me*). Listening, Kitty hears only that God—or the "providence" of the title[5]—has blessed Maurice "with years of happiness and love that can never disappear" and that he considers himself "married" to the lost Lucy (58). Kitty claims at the end that she would have understood if he had only told her all this before but that she simply "lacked the information" (58), the plaintive tag she will repeat when she learns at the dinner party Maurice gives, ostensibly in her honor, that he will marry her student, Jane Fairchild, another golden woman so beautiful that Kitty deems it a concession for her to write anything in her class at all (43).[6] Maurice has the same classic goldenness as Richard Hirst in *The Debut*. Not only does their beauty appeal to all women, but they are both mysteriously touched with Christianity (gauged in terms of "providence" by Maurice). Additionally the romantic evocativeness of Richard's ulcer is paralleled by the tragic love story of Maurice. The particular combination of beauty and physical or spiritual maiming is irresistible, we are to believe, to women, or so Kitty thinks; another character in the novel, Pauline, proves her wrong on this count too.

Like a Barbara Pym spinster, Kitty allows herself to be used by Maurice, though with much more serious implications than in the Pym world, where the "victim" eventually becomes humorously indignant.[7] Kitty types Maurice's notes and offers to go with him to view French cathedrals on the grounds that she can "be useful" to him and "do all the boring things" (22). As literature tries to tell her, men soon tire of women who devote their lives to them and sacrifice all for love; the burden of such sacrifice is too great to be borne. Moreover, Maurice, except perhaps in looks, is not worth the sacrifice, seems even to lack the capacity to feel remorse for her plight after the fashion of Adolphe for Ellénore at the end of Constant's novel. A professor of medieval history, he nonetheless offers "inaccurate but moving insights" ("charismatic shit," according to the Roger Fry Professor of Significant Form) about English cathedrals (18). Kitty disagrees with him often but is too absorbed in her love for him to recognize either his shortcomings or her superior knowledge.

A skeptic herself, though she lights a candle for her mother when she visits a cathedral with Maurice, Kitty tries to find religion to keep pace with the man she wants and goes so far as to ask questions of providence (63) and to open the Bible at random passages for guidance.[8] Unhappily for her, she at length believes that she has succeeded; as she is prepared by her grandmother and by her neighbor Caroline for her lecture but, unbeknown to them, really for the dinner at Maurice's, the images are religious. She is a "lay figure" being "adorned" for her dedication to Maurice, really, as we have known all along, her "sacrifice":

She would have liked to shut her door to Caroline whose intention, she knew, was to oversee every stage of the *ritual*, from the vantage point of a greater

experience of the world. But Kitty also knew that she had her own *ritual* to
follow, and that it was fraught with *superstition,* that if she did not obey her
own imperatives, something would be wrong and the evening would be *ill-
omened.* She could not have said what this *ritual* was, but she perceived that it
was something to do with acknowledgment of the *luck* that had come to her,
that in fact her earlier bewildered searchings and dreads had been neutralized,
sanctioned, that she was no longer a *petitioner,* that plans had been made in
which she had a part. For this supreme leniency on the part of *fate* she did not
know what or whom to thank, but made a polite *obeisance* in the direction of
what she now regarded as *Providence,* and for this, she needed to be alone. (143;
my italics)

What follows, this time unbeknown to Kitty, is two days in her own
Gethsemane, her grandmother's garden, where she awaits the great
moment of the dinner at Richard's and where she sees that the old
world and the old Kitty will pass away to be reborn. It is also the right
time: she is thirty, another evocation of Christ (his age when he began
his ministry). "The time had come to say goodbye to those who had
been with her on the first half of her journey . . . [;] she must now
prepare to live a different sort of life": "She would eat reasonable meals,
she would not panic before her lecture, she would deal sensibly with
everyone, but would not allow anyone to dominate her. She was saying
goodbye to her very pliancy, the quality that had kept her, like her
mother, a girl for far too long" (143–44). The irony of the literary
adept being unwittingly embedded in Christ images is almost more
than the reader can bear, and, as in the previous novel, we must ponder
whether the distance between author and character is too great or,
indeed, not great enough. Kitty seems entirely unconscious of the types
into which she (e.g., spinster, Christ figure) or others (e.g., Maurice as
romantic hero, deliverer, god) slip. For her part, Brookner has to have
been conscious of the applied imagery and, given Kitty's lack of aware-
ness, of the terrible irony. The Brookner world again seems oppres-
sively bleak.

Kitty cannot grasp the similarity between what she supposes the
natural folklore of women and the great stereotypes of literature or
people's misapplied distillations from literature. Examples of these
types abound in the novel, though again we question whether they are
for our edification as readers or for Kitty's. During the crossing of the
Channel to France, when she meets Mr. Pascoe, a schoolmaster escort-
ing a group of students to Italy, she instantly knows that he is aware of
his "Byronic head" and poses it to advantage. When he tells her that he

has a "bad leg," her response (to herself) is immediate and knowledgeable: "That is simply not true thought Kitty. You read that in a novel
about the First World War. She blushed slightly at this evidence of bad
faith on her part" (107). She would enjoy him very much "if only [he]
weren't so impossibly self-absorbed. A Romantic hero, she decided.
And with the limp to go with it" (108). Why, then, is she so blind to
the posing of Maurice and to the stereotype that he is? Why is she so
unable to deal with a central message of *Adolphe* (the novel she is
teaching in her seminar): a man gets tired of a woman sacrificing all for
him? Instead she chooses to have her students analyze the use of the
words in the novel (41).

Brookner herself provides a commentary on her own and the Constant novel. In an interview, she agrees that "although literature can
mislead one, it can also provide moral answers" and then expands on
this view: "*Adolphe* is a deeply serious and moral novel: it asks what do
you do when you are the author of a disaster? Ellénore in *Adolphe* and
Kitty in *Providence* are victims of disasters because they misjudge their
men."[9] What Brookner does not explain, in the interview or in *Providence,* is how Kitty, with so much intellectual equipment and training,
can be so blind. As a novelist in the tradition of Balzac and Flaubert,
she is not obligated to do so, of course, but the accumulation of data
should allow the reader to draw such conclusions and does not.

Kitty Maule suffers a divorce between intellect and emotion that is
foreshadowed by her separation into two names and beings (and perhaps
by the play on *maul* of her last name); she has some grasp of the problem
but never finds the solution for which she hopes: "I function well in one
sphere only, but all the others must be thought through, every day.
Perhaps I will graft myself onto something native here, make a unity
somehow. I can learn. I can understand. I can even criticize. What I
cannot do is reconcile. I must work on that" (52). We begin to suspect,
however, that compartmentalization will remain a way of life and a way
of profession with her. In the whole of the romantic tradition, for
example, she can find only extremes of a continuum (as Brookner's
heroines repeatedly seem to see only opposites, never gradations in
between):

She did not know what she found more impressive: the ability to stagger on
through a life exaggeratedly devoid of normal happiness, or the ability to
admit a radiant fragmentation of the mind that would put one out of the
struggle altogether. What worried her was that there appeared to be no middle

way. She could not accept that so much ardour and longing, so much torment and courage, should peter out into the flatlands of middle and old age. (33)

Yet, countless thousands—romantics and contemporaries—live out their lives without even knowing the extremes of such continua. Brookner does not suggest that her heroines are simply predetermined or fated to fail at life in the terms in which others succeed. They *can* thrust themselves forward into the game. The problem is that they operate from an inchoate perception that they belong to the unfortunate category of the only two large classes of people in existence: the golden and the ordinary, what Margaret Drabble's characters would perceive as the lucky/privileged and the unlucky/unprivileged, carnivores and herbivores. In fact, Drabble's heroines belong to the former category; Brookner's, to the latter, though they have many of the accoutrements of Drabble's privileged; they have learning, are well off, and have good looks (to which they are generally blind). Drabble's characters are unselfish and worry about their good fortune, however, as unfair. Brookner's protagonists are generally self-defeating and nonassertive. As Brookner has said in response to a question about the determinism in *Providence,* "One's character and predisposition determine one's fate, I'm afraid."[10] Insofar as anyone in the world can be free,[11] however, her women could change themselves—if not from moral to selfish, then to something—more human—that combines self and nonself. Not one of them, including Kitty, ever seems to see middle ways.[12]

"The fault [then], Dear [Kitty], is not in our stars, / But in ourselves, that we are [*women*]." What Brookner seems to have been working out in the earlier novels and finally writes large in *The Misalliance* and *A Friend from England* is that "all good fortune is a gift of the gods, and that you don't win the favor of the ancient gods by being good, but by being *bold.*" This clarity comes in response to the following summation by the interviewer:

Your first three novels seem to be variations on the same theme. The basic argument is that we are deceived by literature in believing that virtue is rewarded, that good will win in the end, and that Cinderella will always get the Prince. Whereas, in reality, honest, disciplined and principled people lose to the beautiful and the selfish.[13]

Brookner substitutes *plausible* for *selfish* in the interview and *viable* (and *viability*) throughout the novels. Because they do not win the expected

reward for their good behavior and the expected prince that literature
and feminine lore have taught them to expect, her heroines feel that
they are nonpersons and, worse, that some great personal lack is responsible for their failures.

Kitty, like Ruth Weiss of *The Debut,* undervalues her own talents
because she finds her work so easy and must expend more time to serve
a special dish for Maurice than to write a paper or prepare for one of her
seminars. She wants her lecture on the romantic tradition to be excellent in order to please Maurice. When it is over, she has "a sense of
well-being and *almost of worth*" (173; my italics). Well launched in her
career from our point of view, she exists in a temporary state, waiting
and wanting to live with someone [really Maurice] so that she "can
begin" her life (58). Simultaneously she admits to recovering her earlier
feelings of safety, from the period before the abrupt death of her
mother, when she is "among her books" (59). Her view of the gifts love
bestows could come straight from the romantic literature she teaches,
and the only reason she can find for her lack of love is self-flaws:

The love of one person for another can confer such a charmed life that even the
memory of it bestows immunity [a lesson to be gleaned also, as Kitty believes,
from the communion between Maurice and Lucy].[14] She herself was not immune. And if she had one wish, it was to know that immunity, to be loved in
such a way that even when parted from the other she would never be alone. She
wondered if there were anything in her life, in herself, that could make her
lovable in that way, and realized that there was nothing, not even a basis for
comparison. Perhaps it was because she lacked faith, as Maurice said, that she
was tense, that she could not take life more easily, that she could not take him
for granted. For surely, they were dearest friends? Surely, he would not talk as
he had talked tonight to anyone else? (59)

Kitty is also blind to her own physical beauty and primarily because
she cuts the world of women into two halves: the have's like Jane
Fairchild and the have-nots like herself. She assumes that she is not
among the category known as beautiful women: "Beauty, of course,
offered its own dispensations: beautiful women, by a rule she acknowledged but did not understand, were somehow allowed to do nothing of
worth and yet to command the time and attention of others" (29). She
knows that she is "lucky" to attract a man like Maurice (22), though
she is very attractive. What others tell us about her is that she just
needs to "take herself in hand." Pauline reminds us of a truism ("*Jour-*

nalière, that used to be called," according to Mrs. Bentley): "[Kitty] looks very pretty when she is animated and rather plain when she is not" (150). Caroline, at one end of a continuum, with female dons on the other, reaches the same conclusion: "The thing is, Kitty, that you sometimes look a bit depressed, if you don't mind my saying so. As if you've . . . I don't know, been stood up or something" (154). The irony of the portrait is again uppermost; as Kitty, who sees no middle ways, is *a* romantic and *no* romantic, so she is *a* beauty and *no* beauty, *a* clotheshorse and *no* clotheshorse.

Foil Characters and Continua

In *Providence,* Brookner again relies on foils and again calls attention to their use. Unusually, moreover, they are closely bound up with the whole question of the influence of literature on life, especially on the lives of the heroine and of other women. As a scholar of literature, Kitty is familiar with the technique of foil characters. What is really being developed here, however, is the question of how, with her knowledge, she can be so taken in by and so naive about love and its entanglements. We continue to have the impression of a sharp divorce between literature on the page, at whose analysis Kitty is an adept, and life, another echo of *The Debut.* At most, she seems to pluck verbal tags (e.g., "wise passiveness" [37]; "assumption of effortlessness" [38]; "strategy of elegance" [38]) from her literary analysis and try to live by them. We continue to ask how a woman this intelligent professionally can be so dismally ignorant of human relationships that involve herself, especially when she is well aware of the sexual games women like her neighbor Caroline Costigan play. A divorcée known for her orange hair[15] and very high heels, Caroline can walk as well as anyone else but leans on Kitty and uses her "as a convenient *foil* in the absence of a man" (67; my italics).

At least Kitty does not choose Caroline as a model. Though she believes that she herself lacks "some essential feminine quality" residing "in the folklore passed on by women who possessed a knowledge that she was forced to supplement by reading books" and has secretly studied advice columns and horoscopes for answers (66), she sees that Caroline's "knowledge" has gone wrong. She must live frugally on her alimony and consults fortune-tellers for when her "luck" will change. Nonetheless, Kitty does not seem to see the parallel between Caroline's dressing each day and shopping in Harrods or sitting in restaurants to

pass the time and her own frenetic walks and rituals, and she too comes
to participate in the fortune-telling.

Kitty is offered a continuum of women in the novel, though she
again discounts the possibility of learning through them and merely
recognizes how tired she gets of women's company (153). At one end,
Caroline is woman as hunter, and she tries to share her wiles of makeup
and dress with Kitty, to no avail. At the other end is woman as don
and, from Kitty's point of view at least, liberated woman of the "kind
envied by captive housewives" (80): Pauline Bentley, who teaches in the
Romance Languages Department at Kitty's university. She is a "thin
clever woman" in tweed suits, who reminds Kitty "of what awaited her
if her life failed to change. Pauline was a gifted and honourable teacher
but she was admired rather than liked, for years of hiding her feelings
had made her sarcastic, unsentimental, in a way that was good for
departmental efficiency but bad for students looking for the sort of
glamorous governess figure they were prepared to tolerate in a female
tutor" (78). She goes home every night to a small cottage in Glouces-
tershire with an old dog and a nearly blind mother, a former distinguished don, who thinks that her daughter is not ambitious enough.
Pauline, Kitty believes, is too bright not to know her fate, and her
mother knows it too and exacts from Kitty a promise that, when Mrs.
Bentley dies, she will make Pauline use her inheritance to travel around
the world. Both her mother and Kitty assume that Pauline is also in
love with Maurice, but she claims always to have disliked him. Her
ability to assess his character could be a legacy for Kitty, but she
remains frozen in her either-or stance and does not glean the good from
the less good in the portraits before her:

> She felt an urgent need to put her own life into some sort of order, to ensure
> that she did not turn out like Caroline or like Pauline, the one so stupid,[16] the
> other so intelligent, and both so bereft. She saw her two friends, who would
> have nothing to say to each other if they should ever meet, as casualties of the
> same conflict, as losers in the war in which Providence was deemed to play so
> large a part, and to determine the outcome, for some, not for others. (81)

Here she not only submits our outcomes to determinism but, in reject-
ing both portraits, falls back into the old trap of being unable to
reconcile. Ironically she will later give the lie to this approach when she
imagines a different fate for Pauline: "She will be all right, she decided.
She will see the world, that I guarantee. She will marry a retired

colonial official and settle down in Hong Kong. I shall hear from her once a year—a letter inside a Christmas card, ending 'George joins me in sending his warmest wishes'. I see it clearly" (87). At various junctures in the novels, Brookner's heroines see the future for others in utter (and believable) clarity, as Rachel imagines what will happen to Michael and his father in *A Friend from England,* but they remain unimaginative about and even blind to their own possibilities. Kitty's obtuseness is also revealed by her acknowledgment, in the passage just quoted, of providence, in which she is seeking to believe, as well as by her failure to recognize the necessity for taking one's destiny into one's own hands.

Persistently in the novel, Kitty acts only in response to a precipitating action of someone else. For example, when she receives a postcard from Maurice, she is so exhilarated that she takes her grandparents out for the first time in years. They too are foils, but she is unaware of them as such and has dismissed them as something she needs to hide and keep from her English life precisely in order to have an English life. She does not recognize that her grandmother's making of dresses for her on special occasions has always been Louise's own cherished ritual of family continuity, one "so familiar as to be unnoticeable" (136). And the epiphany or vignette that occurs in the taxi is very like, though in reverse of meaning, that in James's *The Ambassadors* when Lambert Strether sees the Countess de Vionnet and Chad on the shore and knows instantly that they are lovers. This one is meaningful principally for Vadim and Louise (and will be replayed in Oscar and Dorrie of *A Friend from England*): " 'Would you like to walk a bit?' [Kitty] asked. They did not answer. Their hands were tightly entwined. *'Tu te souviens, ma Louise?'* murmured Vadim. 'Everything,' said Louise, in a voice that Kitty had never heard before. 'I remember everything' " (96). If Kitty wants an image of love, she has just found it in the world she rejects. Ironically her French grandmother is able to speak in English and her Russian grandfather in French at a moment of great emotional communion. Kitty maintains separate and distinguished worlds always. Almost as if in punishment, she will have to take instant and awful meaning from the vignette at the end of the novel when Maurice and "Miss Fairchild" take their places at the head and foot of the dinner table. Louise is even able to recognize the "signs of love" in her granddaughter:

The desire to please, the preoccupation at the back of the eyes, the voluntary half-smile. And the watchfulness, the control. The determination to make the

most out of what might be very little. And the evenings when she telephoned
very early, as if to get the call out of the way. Louise sensed the love in her
grand-daughter [*sic*], although it seemed to her without an object. No name
had been mentioned, no confidences exchanged. (98–99)

In this pair is the wisdom Kitty is seeking. It is not to be found just in
the womenlore that she thinks is mysteriously passed down from one
woman to the next, excepting only her, and not merely in even the best
of literature. With irony again, Brookner has had Kitty play off the
naturalness of Maurice (which we know as artifice) against her own
artificiality; all the while her grandparents are the most natural of all in
the novel and thus the best foils for their granddaughter's inspection.
Instead she has rather "romantically" followed the pattern of Dante's
Paolo and Francesca, though their lust leads to murder. [17] "Reading
interrupted by kissing and followed by death seemed to her an entirely
natural progression" (89).

In spite of the many signs provided for her along the way and her
persisting denseness, we continue to feel that Kitty is severely treated
by Brookner, who seems to want to offer her up as proof that no human
successes are proof against an unrelenting world in which no one can
be, ultimately, free. Thus Kitty must pay a sharp penalty for her
obtuseness. At every instance when she thinks that luck is hers and she
has Maurice at last, irony takes over. She has pined away for him in
France, doing little but waiting for his call. He arrives, and she is
happy just to feed him and let him eat for them both. Suddenly he tells
her that he is going home in the morning. Still, visiting cathedrals that
one day they have together, she lulls herself into believing that their
separation is at fault: "But I am mad, she thought. It is simply that our
earlier unity was broken. This is quite natural. People take some time
to come together again" (121). He leaves without even sleeping with
her.

Brookner also uses foils within foils, artfully playing off Mrs. Bentley and Pauline against the mother and daughter Kitty sees in the
public garden. In the latter pair, the daughter, aged by bitterness over
her lot, looks almost as old as her mother. Neither has ever pleased the
other, and they quickly flee the garden as too hot, leaving "a wake of
bitterness, a dark stain on the bright day" (91). Instead of thinking of
the accepting and acceptable adjustment of the Bentleys, however,
Kitty uses this pair to fuel her desperation to have Maurice:

Maurice took on a superhuman, almost a metaphysical significance for Kitty. His brilliance and ease, his seeming physical invulnerability, the elevated character of his decisions, the distances he covered, his power of choice and strength of resolve, cast him in the guise of the unfettered man, the mythic hero, the deliverer. For the woman whom Maurice would deliver would be saved for ever from the fate of that grim daughter, whose bare white legs and dull shoes, designed perhaps for some antediluvian hike or ramble, continued to register in Kitty's mind's eye. Maurice's choice would be spared the humiliations that lie in wait for the unclaimed woman. She would have a life of splendour, raising sons. Ah! thought Kitty with anguish, the white wedding, the flowers. How can it be me? How could it be me? (91)[18]

The Novel as Novel

As in the first novel, verbal circularity brings an imposed order as *Providence* opens and closes with Kitty Maule's reciting the compressed version of her background that she dares to disclose: "My father was in the army. He died before I was born" (5, 183). The effect is to suggest that the only change wrought by the experiences described in the novel is, as in the case of Ruth Weiss, a passive acceptance of the life that has been dealt out. Ruth and Kitty will live in the success of their professional lives only. Both books succeed as well-written and minute character studies. The fact that one heroine ends not only married but widowed and still unhappy and unsuccessful in her own eyes, while the other ends unmarried and still unhappy and unsuccessful in her own eyes confirms us in the recognition that Brookner is not confining herself to a portrayal, for example, of spinsters, however different hers might be in delineation from those of Barbara Pym. The great flaw—here and in most of the rest of Brookner's work—is that the heroines flounder amid authorial cues that seem to be present primarily for our benefit, as if the writer were saying to her heroines, "I have given you all the pieces of the puzzle; if you cannot figure out the answers, I am not to blame. After all, I started from a similar position, and just 'look at me.' " Brookner denies such an interpretation, of course: "I hope I am not an aggressive writer, and that I see through people with compassion and humor. My own life was disappointing—I was *mal partie* (started on the wrong footing); so I am trying to edit the whole thing."[19]

This novel stands out for its playfully acidic portrayals of academic "administrivia"[20] and infighting; its characterizations of Caroline, Pauline, and, especially, the aged Mrs. Bentley;[21] and its control by strong chains of food[22] and of religious imagery. Perhaps the real achievement of *Providence,* however, is that, for all of her stupidity about affairs of the heart, her blindness to Maurice's flaws, and her willingness to be used, Kitty continues to engage our attention, compassion, and interest.

Chapter Four

Look at Me: "No Voice at the World's Tribunals"

Brooknerian Fare but with Variations

Look at Me (1983), Brookner's third novel but published in the United States before her second, *Providence,*[1] is a first-person account by Frances Hinton, a reference librarian in a medical research institute (specializing, ironically, in human behavior), of her falling in with a golden couple, Nick and Alix Fraser, who also bring James Anstey into the circle as her escort and then exclude her. Frances fights back by trying to consummate her liaison with James, who rejects her for the flagrantly sexual Maria. The greatest irony of the novel is that, thought virginal by Alix and the others, Frances has actually had a devastating love affair that has resulted in such reticence and denial as to suggest pathology and aberration. By her own admission an observer and one famous for her control, Frances is no match for this fast set. Well off financially and ensconced in a large flat with the family maid, Nancy, she works because she wants to and still cannot escape the "Public Holiday Syndrome" that besets those unencumbered by family. Before she died, Mrs. Hinton encouraged her daughter to become a writer by capitalizing on the daily routine of the library and turning it to comedy. In addition to her work and her writing, Frances spends her time in good deeds (e.g., visiting Miss Morpeth, her predecessor), that Brooknerian refuge for the lonely and the dispossessed (like Blanche Vernon in *The Misalliance*). At the end, after suffering a collapse of sorts, she recognizes that she will never be viable enough for those in Alix's circle and retreats to recover, to write, and to accept her diminished lot, which is akin to that of those she has helped. She could marry the brother of her friend Olivia but will not. She feels that her only route to being a person of substance is through writing; if the world will not recognize her as an individual, it will look at her as an author.

Many verbal echoes of or variations on the first two novels appear in

Look at Me. The true non-Englishman here (though Frances feels the usual "disenfranchisement") is Dr. Joseph Simek, a Czech or a Pole with a past as tormenting as that of Mrs. Weiss in *The Debut* and surely a glance at Brookner's Polish family. Kitty Maule's interest in fortune-telling and the psychic recurs in Mrs. Halloran, who "claims to be in touch with the other side" and writes articles for psychic magazines and, on a more significant level, in the strange images that Frances believes conjured up by her mind. As in the first two novels, people offer gratuitous comments on the heroine's looks. Her Aunt Julia has told Frances that she will be unpopular because she normally looks disdainful (a variation on Kitty's "disappointed"), and Frances agrees (175). She receives the usual help, this time from Alix, with her looks and clothes and is unreligious like Kitty in *Providence*.

Frances yields to the charm of the male of the golden pair, Nick Fraser, as easily as Kitty Maule, of *Providence,* to Maurice, though Nick is not her love interest. Without the religious bent of Maurice and of Richard Hirst of *The Debut,* he is yet "distinguished by that grace and confidence of manner that ensure success. He is tall and fair, an athlete, a socialite, well-connected, good-looking, charming: everything you could wish for in a man" (11). Recognizing his flaws (e.g., his careless treatment of Miss Morpeth and Dr. Simek), she nonetheless is glad to work for him and constantly carries the photographs he requests to him and lets him get by with using the diminutive she hates because it is part of "my darling Fanny," the tag her mother used to apply to her.[2]

The female half of the golden pair, Nick's wife, Alix, is much more prominent than in the previous novels. Husband and wife let others pay for their meals, as we have come to expect, but Alix takes the golden woman type further to become herself a predator, enduring her own life by evoking complication and the lurid in those around her, making the outré a quest. As one critic says, "For all her need to be noticed [a reference to the title], [Frances] is not quite hungry enough, not like Alix Forbes [*sic*], who eats people. Those who continue to interest or amuse her are digested; the rest Alix spits out. Frances, or Little Orphan Fanny as Alix calls her, gives her a few months of good chewing."[3] As in *The Debut* and *Providence,* Brookner uses food imagery in *Look at Me,* for example in Frances's response to Alix and Nick: "So stunning was their physical presence, one might almost say their physical triumph, that I immediately felt weak and pale, not so much decadent as *undernourished, unfed* by life's more potent forces, condemned to dark rooms, and *tiny meals,* and an obscure creeping existence which would be appropriate to my enfeebled status and which would allow me gently to decline into extinction" (37; my italics). Again Brookner mixes metaphorical and literal in a way that constantly suggests her heroines' obsessive focus on the relation between all experience and themselves.

Brookner also has Alix, Nick, and Frances function as Helen, George, and Mrs. Cutler in *The Debut* but with essential differences. Instead of the outsider (Mrs. Cutler) being "one of those *louche* women who thrive on the intimacy of couples" (*Debut,* 21; my italics), the couple is the user:

What interested me far more, although I also found it repellent, was their intimacy as a married couple. I sensed that it was in this respect that they found my company necessary: they exhibited their marriage to me, while sharing it only with each other. I soon learned to keep a pleasant noncommittal smile on my face when they looked into each other's eyes, or even caressed each other; I felt lonely and excited. I was there because some element in that perfect marriage was deficient, because ritual demonstrations were needed to maintain a level of arousal which they were too complacent, perhaps too spoilt, even too lazy, to supply for themselves, out of their own imagination. I was the *beggar at their feast,* reassuring them by my very presence that they were richer than I was. Or indeed could ever hope to be. (57; my italics)

Brookner even reuses the word *louche* as she has Frances imagine an affair between Alix and James: "The novelist in me took over for a moment, and I plotted the whole thing out; then I accused myself of the most suspect form of calculation—crude, louche, cynical—and I dismissed the whole fantasy" (76). The irony is that Frances blames her writer's eye for the off-color when her value to Alix resides in the proportion of the off-color that can be extracted from Frances. Perhaps an even greater irony resides in the fact that Frances has already experienced the louche in the only real affair she has and one not awful just because the man was already married:

I have said that I did not love [James] in the fatal sense. By that I mean that he was not a drug, an obsession, like that time of which I never speak. I did not have to strive for his attention, I did not have to abandon everything when he appeared, I did not have to squander all my resources at a sign from him. In fact, after the debasement of that previous time, I experienced with James a renewal of innocence, and I felt more at home with that innocence than with that cynicism of desire and contempt so strangely mingled that I had previ-

ously known. That secrecy, that urgency, that bitterness, that lack of
hope. . . . I had enjoyed the openness of consorting with an eligible man (how
prehistoric that sounds!) in full view of others, after those stratagems and those
returns in the early hours of the morning, weeping, my coat huddled round
me to conceal the clothes so hastily put on and now creased. The concealed
pain, the lying morning face. I could not go through that again. (121–22)

The greatest irony of the book is that Alix is absolutely right: Frances
does conceal information, only it is not information about the uncon-
summated union with James Anstey but about that earlier union,
which was more corrupt than can be imagined by Alix, who remains,
after all, faithful to her husband however much she may try to convey a
taint of corruption. Alix is corrupt in word only, though she tries to
encourage corruption in others. Frances "the innocent" has known debasement; the affair with James, which Alix has promoted in order to
observe and enjoy the salacious and what she assumes will be Frances's
loss of innocence, converts Frances to a regained state of innocence in
matters sexual. At the same time, in Frances's perversion of literature
to lure audiences into a facile enjoyment that denies the truth of the
human situation—and particularly of *her* human situation—she is as
much a predator as Alix. Both women make that term a dark contrast
with its almost playful use in Margaret Drabble's *A Summer Bird-Cage,*
in which the "herbivores" who are "preyed upon" are "frumpy" at most.
     Another point of departure in this novel is the fact that Frances also
uses Alix, a fact she would certainly deny, though she observes Alix as
Alix observes her; moreover, she will use her observations in the novel
that she determines to write about her experiences with Alix's group.
She claims that the world is made up of observers and participants in
life's feast and that she belongs to the ranks of the former. Alix,
however, is both, and Frances tries to be both. She is also condescending and more so than Kitty Maule talking about the "stupidity" of
Caroline Costigan in *Providence.* She knows, for example, that the beautiful people have "very limited" attention spans (15) and enters into a
conspiracy with Nick to keep up Alix's spirits and keep her off the two
subjects that send her into dispair: how she has come down in the world
with the loss of her father's estate in Jamaica and how cold it is. In fact,
pretending to be uncritical, she is anything but that. If the Frasers
laugh at the glass birds and the ashtrays inherited with the Hintons's
apartment, Frances thinks little of the few pieces of furniture that Alix

has salvaged from her former home. Indeed Alix is taken in by Frances, for she lacks the qualities she is assumed to have:

> Yet I was in my way necessary. I was an audience and an admirer; I relieved some of her frustration: I shared her esteem for her own superiority; and I was loyal and well-behaved and totally uncritical. Yet she found me dull, intrinsically dull, simply because I was loyal and well-behaved and uncritical. And I knew that she would always prefer people like her friend Maria, whom she could insult and scandalize, whom she would defame and snub, only to have it all done back to her by Maria. This provided her with a sort of excitement which I found rather tedious. (56–57)

The verbal tag that Frances borrows from Nick for Alix, "she who must be obeyed" (e.g., 54, 93, 120), is both humorous[4] and deflating. We have difficulty seeing Alix as a femme fatale after such treatment.

Most of Brookner's heroines have some funding to enable them to be independent, but Frances is the richest to date. Her father inherited a toy factory, sold it, invested in the stock market with his friend, Sydney Goldsmith, and became wealthy. Long since dead, he left Frances and her mother in a large flat the Hintons had taken when he had to be in London during the war. After a lingering illness, Mrs. Hinton died (some two years before the novel opens), and Frances is isolated, alone in the large flat whose furnishings were left behind by the previous tenants, with the aging maid. A standard Brooknerian heroine, she cannot assert herself enough to have Nancy stop serving every night the same meal that she would have prepared for Frances's mother. She escapes by working; she does not want to go home, puts off doing so as long as she can, and, like her sisters, Ruth Weiss and Kitty Maule of *The Debut* and *Providence,* respectively, walks in all weather to purge her "restlessness" and "tendency to brood" (18). With Kitty, she knows that hers is a dull life for one so young, and her only salvation is her writing, which, although it dispels her heaviness and charges her "with a kind of electricity," ultimately leads to greater restlessness (18). Very much in the vein of Barbara Pym's characters, she detests Sundays and "all those terrible public holidays" when she can "never, ever, find an adequate means of using up all the available time" (70), particularly Christmas, and she likes Monday mornings, when she can go back to work. More poignantly than Pym, she recalls seeing the well dressed in the launderette on Christmas to avoid being alone, "reduced to spend-

ing their day like this, and finding what company the desperation of
others afforded them" (153). Much less well off than Frances, Mrs.
Halloran and Dr. Simek come to the library because it is warm, and the
former, who lives in a private hotel in South Kensington, is forced to
get out during the day.

Luck and the Writer's Craft

Look at Me has the accustomed complement of luck too—the luck of
others predominantly and the feeling, launched particularly in *Providence,* that some are chosen to be among the lucky, with those unchosen
able to do nothing on their own behalf. The variation of this novel is
that luck becomes bound up with the craft of writing. Frances feels
lucky not to dream and to have good health but resents being referred
to as looking healthy. She feels lucky to have been taken into the
enchanted circle of the Frasers and is actually unlucky on that count.
Perhaps the most disconcerting fact about Brooknerian heroines, indeed, is that we begin to anticipate disappointment and catastrophe as
soon as they mention feeling lucky. No matter how worthy they are,
they never believe—or believe in—their own worth, as in the case with
Kitty in *Providence,* only their luck, an assurance of which they seek to
excess and aberration. Frances knows that luck is the secret at the heart
of the success of the golden people:

Once I followed a girl in the street simply because she looked so lucky that I
could not tear myself away from her. Apart from her youth and her beauty, she
had the sort of assurance that promised well for her, as if her expectations were
so high, so naturally high, that she had set a standard for herself that others
would be encouraged to reach. She seemed to await the best of everything, and
I remember staring at her as if she had decended from another planet. Being an
observer in these matters does not always help one. Sometimes the scenes and
people one observes impart their own message of exclusion. And yet the
fascination of the rare perfect example persists, and it demands that one lay
down one's pen and stalk it, study it, dissect it, learn it, love it. That was how
I felt when I first saw Alix with Nick. I knew that I could never learn enough
about them, but also that I might never understand what I learned. Therefore
I watched them with particular care. (42)

If Margaret Drabble's characters are embarrassed because they are lucky,
Brookner's women believe themselves damned because they are unlucky
and damn themselves by so believing; if they have been relegated to the

ranks of the unlucky, they see no likelihood for change based on individual initiative. Frances concludes that the only reason she is a writer is her lack of luck to be born lucky:

> And I did not write for many evenings that followed [the beginning of the relationship with James]. In my new security I began to see it all in a different light. I began to hate that inner chemical excitement that made me run the words through in my head while getting ready to set them down on the page; I felt a revulsion against the long isolation that writing imposes, the claustration, the sense of exclusion; I experienced a thrill of distaste for the alternative life that writing is supposed to represent. It was then that I saw the business of writing for what it truly was and is to me. It is *your penance for not being lucky*. It is an attempt to reach others and to make them love you. It is *your instinctive protest, when you find you have no voice at the world's tribunals, and that no one will speak for you.* (84; my italics)

Not the least of the problems here is that Frances, like most other Brookner women, again sees only either-or alternatives. Her view of the writer and of writing is derivative and stereotypical: writing is isolation.

Frances apparently represents the view of writing held by Brookner herself prior to working through to new meaning by her fiction. In response to an interviewer's comment that "In *Look At Me* you say that writing is your penance for not being lucky," Brookner says:

> I meant that writing is a very lonely activity. You go for days without seeing or talking to anyone. And all the time out there people are living happy, fulfilled lives—or you think they are. If I were happy, married with six children, I wouldn't be writing. And I doubt if I should want to. But since I wrote that sentence I have changed. Now I write because I enjoy it. Writing has freed me from the despair of living. I feel well when I am writing; I even put on a little weight!

The interviewer also points out Brookner's claim in *Look at Me* to "write to be hard, to remind people that you are there," another justification for the title of the novel but a view about which Brookner has subsequently also changed her mind: "Far from making me hard, writing has made me softer, more understanding, more observant, and perhaps more passive in the sense that other people and their opinion of me seems [*sic*] to matter less."[5] With the possible exception of "more observant," Frances has not yet made these gains through her writing. What is more, although she is a virtual beginner, with only two stories published, we have difficulty imagining that she will move so far because we have difficulty accepting her descriptions of how funny her material is. As Anne Duchêne points out, the novel "moves between two extreme focal lengths: one reflecting a very precise and elegant sardonic microcosm, the other a sea of raging private misery. It takes rather longer, as the author intends it should, to appreciate its full irony—that the unhappiness which first engages our sympathy should finally forfeit it."[6]

Autobiography seems to play a customary hand in this third novel but not in the same way as formerly. If Brookner has to some extent provided alter egos previously, now, in writing a novel largely about writing, she is surely speaking about her own craft and career.[7] One interesting difference between Frances and the first two Brookner women also relates to her being a writer. In contrast to Kitty Maule, she never dreams; the transmittal of knowledge from her unconscious occurs, rather, through images that surface and resubmerge. Brookner for the first time openly explores the operation of her heroine's unconscious—one of the ways by which Frances says "Look at me!"—through images that combine memory and conjuration, as in the following:

The image sprang up in my mind: Sydney proffering his lavish box of chocolates, Nancy in tears, a lace handkerchief of my mother's (for I gave her most of the things) pressed to her mouth. I could not quite dismiss this image, although I had conjured it up. It did not strike me until much later that this scene, which was so vivid to me, had not yet taken place. I saw no significance in the fact that this episode, pieced together from elements observed at disparate moments (the box of chocolates from many previous occasions, the tears from yet another), seemed to be a memory but was in fact a conjuration. The fact that two sets of time had come together in this way I accepted as perfectly normal. (71)

Brookner's novels frequently use leitmotifs, and *Look at Me* has two predominant ones, both related to writing. One is that of the title, and it recurs some seven times, its initial context (15) suggesting Frances's addiction to the lucky golden people who are phenomena in their own right, despite lacking intrinsic merit, and from whom she seeks recognition and notice, though knowing that they will eventually leave her realm. They have a marvelous destiny in store, and she loves their entire lives, which will be so different from her own. If she were lucky enough to have their looks and manner, she could attract attention; as it is, she can only exert herself through writing that removes from her characters "all the sadness that [she] might feel in [her]self" (19) and makes her audience laugh. She claims that she really "found out about writing," that is, found out that it could make others look at her, when she showed James the "prestigious American magazine" in which one of her short stories was published. He was delighted: "That smile was directed at the magazine, which he held in his hands, and I knew then that I wanted that smile to be directed nowhere but at myself. Look at me, I wanted to say, look at me" (85). Her debasement of writing is thus established early in the novel, for hers will hide the truth about life and merely amuse for the primary purpose of calling attention to herself.

Frances forges the link between writing and self-notice that was to be predicted from the opening for the novel (another exceptionally fine one), the second great leitmotif. If less prominent and obvious, it is more gnomic and relates to the subtexture of images and conjuration of the emergent writer, as well as to the secret maiming of Frances: "Once a thing is known it can never be unknown. It can only be forgotten. And, in a way that bends time, so long as it is remembered, it will indicate the future. It is wiser, in every circumstance, to forget, to cultivate the art of forgetting. To remember is to face the enemy. The truth lies in remembering" (5). We are not surprised, then, by her admission:

> I would give my entire output of words, past, present, and to come, in exchange for easier access to the world, for permission to state "I hurt" or "I hate" or "I want."[8] Or, indeed, "Look at me." And I do not go back on this. For once a thing is known it can never be unknown. It can only be forgotten. And writing is the enemy of forgetfulness, or thoughtlessness. For the writer there is no oblivion. Only endless memory. (84)

When the break with James and the Frasers is under way, Frances is forced to focus her need to be looked at on James, who, at lunch with her, is clearly uneasy and wishes to avoid eye contact. Instead of clearing the air, the meeting clouds the relationship more, and she is no more capable of talking out the problem with James than of delivering information to Alix. In some strange way, Frances, with her sister sufferers in Brookner's novels, worries most about being viable,[9] a condition she has apparently enjoyed prior to the love affair that has so altered her and one she stands to regain through James. All evidence to the contrary notwithstanding, most women, Brookner says again, expect to get to the ball with Cinderella:

Once I had great confidence, great cheerfulness; I did not question my purpose or the purpose of others. All that had gone, and I had done my best to replace it. I had become diligent instead of spontaneous; I had become an observer when I saw that I was not to be allowed to participate. I had refused to be pitiable. I had never once said, Look at me. Now, it seemed, I must make one more effort, one more attempt to prove myself viable. And if I succeeded, I might be granted one more opportunity to do it all over again. I did not dare to think what would happen if I failed. (123–24)

In contrast, Kitty Maule expected to gain viability for the first time when Maurice chose her, and we have no indication that either Kitty or Ruth Weiss will try again.

We begin to suspect that the truest statement in Frances's outpourings is her recognition that her writing hides, by producing the antithesis of, her real feelings. The great crisis of her life has been that "debasement," her term (121). As a result, the persona she adopts and the literature she writes are for the purpose of self-concealment; she pleads to be looked at but only as the author of the text on the page, the only text she can control. Ironically, the ongoing subconscious work of her conjuration and unbidden images indicates that her control, too, is illusory.

The circularity of *Providence* (Kitty's intoning of her father's story revealing stasis rather than growth) is repeated here as a structural device to give unity and is actually more carefully conceived. Instead of appearing at the opening this time, the tag that is repeated at the end of the novel, "My Darling Fan," spoken by Mrs. Hinton as she motivated Frances to become a writer, is deferred to page 16 but has been prepared for in the opening lines of the novel. If Ruth Weiss returns "home to her father"[10] in *The Debut,* Frances, having strayed from the call to be a writer by succumbing to the charms of the Frasers, symbolically returns "home to her mother" by moving into her mother's bedroom and by remembering Mrs. Hinton's voice at the end of the novel. We find it hard to believe, however, that she will be the successful woman her mother was in terms of her relation to her husband, her lasting friendships, and the admiration she has evoked. On one level, Frances has learned on her job in the library:

I even try to work out some of the pictures [photographs of doctors and patients through the ages, but especially depictions of melancholy and madness] for myself. I find the power of images very strong, even when I do not understand them. Sometimes an image stands for something that will only be understood in due course. It is a mnemonic, a cryptogram, very occasionally a token of precognition. I pay very great attention to images, both at the Library and away from it. I spend a lot of time on my own, and the contents of my mind, which is nothing out of the ordinary, amaze me with their random significance. That is why I like the Library, not only for the task of classification which is its main purpose, but for the potency of its images, like the Fool on the Tarot Card, or Melancholia with her torn book, or Goya with his doctor. (17)

Frances's life, then, is straining toward a pattern through her unconscious and is straining to contain the oppositions that she and other Brookner women see as the givens of life. What kind of will can encompass classification and randomly flung forth images, love as debasement and love unfelt but needed as a key for regaining viability, writing that both draws on the human scene and lies about it? While Frances is claiming that "one needs to be as cunning as Ulysses in order to negotiate one's own passage" and that she will write herself "into a new way of life" (31), her inner self is writing her life into the mold of the old world of the flat. She can write down every quirk of behavior around her (31) and study human behavior at work, but hers is going to be the same "antique pattern" justified, finally by her, as what one gives up to be a writer. Ruth Weiss did not learn from French literature; Kitty Maule did not learn from romantic literature; Frances Hinton does not learn from "human behavior."

When Alix first comes to the library, Frances's unconscious is already working. Two images beset her, the first of Dr. Constantine begging over the telephone for a hospital bed for her dying mother. What impresses her about the scene is that he is begging and that he is "without resource" (45), her own case when she is cast off by the Frasers and James. This image probably haunts her because she, in contrast to Nancy and Dr. Constantine, has seemed unmoved at her mother's death (as Ruth Weiss has been stoical at the death of her grandmother) and because her unconscious sends it as a warning of what is ahead. The second image, "for no reason that [she] can identify" (45), is of her father's rosewood cigarette box that she played with as a child and only now, in the image, recognizes as flawed.

Frances prides herself on being a student of the "sub-text" (74) but consistently misunderstands her own subtext, her unconscious self, as well as the subterranean workings of those around her; thus she ends up like Kitty Maule of *Providence,* who is another close reader of text, both surface and subsurface, though the import of the messages read by the two is quite different. Frances recognizes that she has loved James and admits that "since I had apparently understood so little, I could not even blame him. I get things wrong, you see" (183). Like Kitty, she has simply believed in the relationship because she needed to: "I found such reticence very exciting. For I knew he cared for me" (89). The truth comes imagistically and epiphantically—in vignette—as it came to Kitty when she saw Maurice and Jane take their places at the two ends of the dinner table. In the restaurant, Frances suddenly sees and hears Maria bend over James with food and say, "More, darling. I want you to be good and strong tonight. More" (160). The technique is again Jamesian, if the language is more contemporary and thus less refined.

After James Anstey rejects Frances sexually and she succumbs to an amnesiaclike state akin to that exacted by Blanche Vernon's migraine in *The Misalliance,* images again pursue her. She sees the rosewood box, now very large "because I was so small; I was running a child's hand over the slightly irregular, slightly imperfect edge. I was repeating the gesture over and over again. I had nothing else to do, because I was a child and I was waiting for the adults to come back from what was so mysteriously keeping them and to allow me once again into their company" (131). Reflected in the window are Dr. Constantine, Dr. Simek, Mrs. Halloran, Miss Morpeth, and Frances herself. She has not only been reduced to the status of a child by a supposed lack of sexuality that masks in fact an overdose of aberrant sexuality but has joined the league of those "without resource." We can only hope that as she pursues her writing, she will go back to that image of the ailing and heartsick Dr. Simek, who forced himself to stand and "composed his face into an expression of worldly good humour suitable to leave-taking and inclined his head in farewell. He did not, perhaps could not, shake my hand, but remained braced against the back of his chair, his other hand gripping the amber holder." The image is "so powerful, and so disturbing" that she went home and wrote it down (114). This is where real writing will be found—in the lives of those who struggle on despite being without resource. They throw into relief the fatuousness of Frances's trying to make the human lot merely funny. Perhaps in time, too, she will remember that it is James who told her the tragic details of the lives of Dr. Simek and Dr. Leventhal. She has written a funny short story about the latter and called it "Professor Rosenbaum and the Delphic Oracle"; if she ever reaches the point of thinking about its contrast with the facts of Leventhal's life, it may become "Frances Linton and the Delphic Oracle" and make her really "look at herself."

Foil Characters: Alternative Ways of Living and Loving

In *Providence,* Kitty was largely blind to the poignant pattern of married love set by her grandparents. Two such positive images are presented in *Look at Me* and with as little effect on Frances. Mrs. Hinton has been part of an "antique pattern" (30) in which the men in her life (her husband, Sydney Goldsmith, and Dr. Constantine) "were like priests, ministering to her" and "were kind, shy, easily damaged, too sensitive to her hurts." Mr. Hinton "was mainly concerned with earning a living in a way which would leave him entirely free to devote himself to" his wife (29). Frances has shied away from such sentiment not because, as is the case with Ruth Weiss, she knows "how easy it was to come by" (*Debut,* 32) but because that first affair was so devastating and has, in her mind's eye, so depraved her. She can never be like her mother or those men who so atypically reveal their emotion. The mistake is that Frances flees to the Frasers and what they represent as a kind of mistaken middle ground between worship (what her mother has experienced at least by Frances's reading) and depravity (what she has experienced):

I wanted an end to shabbiness, to pretence, to anxiety, to dissembling. That last time, the time of which I never speak, had been so unendurable and also so baffling. I had found myself rising, somehow, to expectations which I did not fully understand: grossness, cruelty, deceit. I had been humiliated, and had been enjoyed precisely because I was humiliated. It was all so different from what others had believed of me. I had managed, somehow, to live two lives. But in the end it was the more respectable of those lives that I had inherited. I minded, of course. Oh yes, I minded. But at the same time I knew that whatever people say and whatever they put up with and whatever they get away with, love should be simple. And it is. It is.[11] (122)

Frances is little better than other Brooknerians at finding middle ground; she sees herself as not powerful and thus "able to bend others to

[her] will" and as not "particularly malleable, and therefore able to bend to the will of others" (123). Kitty, we recall, considered herself too pliable. Still, we begin to be more sympathetic toward Frances when we at last learn what she has been subjected to in that unfortunate love affair—the "incalculable" and the "undiagnosed" (5), ironically what the library's collection is weighted toward.

The real middle ground is much healthier. It is represented by Olivia's family, whose members enjoy one another and love Sundays (days dreaded by people like Frances and by Pym spinsters), when they are together. Their contentment spills over to others, and they befriend Frances and her mother. David Benedict, Olivia's lawyer brother, who has secured positions for his sister and Frances in the library, would like to marry her, and their families have wanted the union, but, for whatever obscure reason, Frances will not marry him. We would like to think that her reason, however misguided, has to do with feeling that she is too "shopworn," too "soiled," to inflict herself on David, and it probably does attach to the latent neurosis that has been triggered by that earlier affair. Finally, there is no accounting either for why Olivia and Frances, though "unmarried and childless, and still living in [their] parents' houses," "don't go so far as to create a home away from home" at the library but limit themselves to their Mickey Mouse mugs (46) as their only concession to humanizing the place. As often in this book and Brookner's other novels, we get the impression that much of the misfortune and dissatisfaction is self-made, one result of her constant use of scenes, situations, and images immanent with meaning but from which she constantly withholds explanation.

Individual women provide foils for Frances too. Most situated like her and most positive is Olivia. An automobile accident has left her virtually immobile. Her beautiful head is supported by a neck brace, but she is "never less than totally composed" (15), and her "moral strength never falters" (46). Yet Frances is dismissive of Olivia, while seeing the Frasers as an opportunity to further her education. Since we are never allowed to view the other characters except through the eyes of Frances, who is too misled to be entirely trustworthy on any point, we do not know if Olivia has really succumbed to Nick's charms, as Frances claims. More likely, like Pauline Bentley, who sees through Maurice in *Providence,* she has taken the measure of the golden boy and found him wanting. While succumbing to Alix enough to cancel her plans with Olivia (as Alix will cause them to skip a dinner party to which they have committed and will lie to the hosts that they were lost), she is loyal enough to her sensible friend to remind Alix that Olivia is "only physically crippled" (161). Almost everyone else in the book, including Frances, is crippled spiritually. Olivia's incapacitation not only provides an effective counterpointing of Frances's emotional mutilation but shows a positive approach to being forced to live a diminished life.

Much in the manner of Ruth Weiss in *The Debut*, who is helped to maintain the secrecy of her inner life by a university environment that does not invite confidences and disclosures, Frances sees herself as "famous" for her control: "By a supreme irony, my control is so great that these crises remain unknown to the rest of the world, and so I am thought to be unfeeling. And of course I never speak of them. That would be intolerable. If I ever suffer loneliness it is because I have settled for the harsh destiny of dealing with these matters by myself" (19). Again, she is posturing, for how can she be famous for control if no one knows that she has anything to be controlled about? Moreover, Olivia does know at least something of what goes on with her. She is willing to become involved enough to help Frances find a way to go off with James, though she wants Frances and her brother to marry. She also, without words being exchanged between them, raises a clenched fist to support Frances as she leaves to do battle with Alix for James. Frances nonetheless chooses Alix over Olivia, succumbing to the pattern of the ascendancy of the beautiful person.

Again, Frances, the great observer of life, miscues. The alternatives for her, as she sees them, are Miss Morpeth, Mrs. Halloran, and Nancy, and they are to be avoided by her entry into a fairly casual relationship:

I was not in love with James, but now there was something to get up for in the mornings, other than that withering little routine that would eventually transform me into a version of Miss Morpeth, although I had no niece in Australia who might brighten my last years. Nor would I turn into Mrs. Halloran, still game, but doomed to hopelessness. No glasses of gin for me, no bottle in the wardrobe of a room in a hotel in South Kensington, no evenings lying on the bed dressed in a housecoat too young and too pink, casting superior horoscopes for those who fear the future. With what thankfulness did I register my deliverance from this dread, which had possessed me for as long as I could remember. I breathed more deeply, slept more soundly, ate more heartily, freed from this weight. Nancy's mumblings and shufflings ceased to

bother me, for they no longer represented the shades of the prison house
[another echo of Wordsworth]. (85–86)

What Frances forgets or overlooks is that her money will protect her
from most of the ravages faced by these women, if not from the most
ravaging, loneliness.

Frances also takes too much credit for stage-managing the lives of others through her good works. She thinks that she has arranged to have Mr.
Reardon, the building porter, visit Nancy, but Nancy entertains a number of visitors, former admirers and friends of Mrs. Hinton, who never
find Frances at home but continue to come anyway. Mr. Reardon and his
assistant have apparently passed pleasantries with Nancy before Frances
has taken a hand in the business. The rituals Nancy performs—for
example, "the ritual tray of ritual food" (51)—that so enrage Frances are
ways not merely to pass the days but to consecrate them and to remember
Mrs. Hinton, as the ritual of making dresses for her granddaughter
heightens Maman Louise's sense of family ties in *Providence*. Frances also
prides herself on her monthly visits to Miss Morpeth and will exact, as a
price for being bored by her, putting the old woman in a novel. What she
learns in their last meeting is truth: that Miss Morpeth knows those connected with the library think her merely a boring old woman and that the
only person she cares about is her niece, whom she will never see again because her health will not permit her to fly to Australia. The greatest revelation to Frances, however, is that the two of them have "evidently
thought of each other in exactly the same way" when they purchased the
identical Christmas gift for each other (140). She is offended that Miss
Morpeth has the same image of Frances as Frances of her, for she has never
really believed that she could end up like the Miss Morpeths of the world.
She also makes a vow never to draw attention to herself in that way: crying her need. She prefers the Frasers, who can "bring these unmanageable
emotions down to a level of curiosity, of gratification" in the way that she
will do through writing. Miss Morpeth has become a foil to her not at all
in the way that Frances has anticipated. Again Frances is learning a new
conception of what it means to "look at me," but we are left to wonder if
she will ever find the middle way between such extremes.

Brookner and Men: A Feminist and No Feminist

For a work centered on so self-centered a heroine, *Look at Me* offers
some intriguing reversals on the man-woman relationship. Men (for

example, the circle around Mrs. Hinton) certainly receive more sympathetic treatment than women (with the exceptions of Nancy and Olivia), at least from the author's point of view, if not the protagonist's. Frances learns at work, for example, that love melancholy can beset men as well as women, though she suspects posing and artifice:

And should melancholy strike a man it will be because he is suffering from romantic love: he will lean his padded satin arm on a velvet cushion and gaze skywards under the nodding plume of his hat, or he will grasp a thorn or a nettle and indicate that he does not sleep. These men seem to me to be striking a bit of a pose, unlike the women, whose melancholy is less picturesque. The women look as if they are in the grip of an affliction too serious to be put into words. The men, on the other hand, appear to have dressed up for the occasion, and are anxious to put a noble face on their suffering. Which shows that nothing much has changed since the sixteenth century, at least in that respect. (6–7)

Frances admits that men can suffer but like Kitty cannot eschew those who are types and so falls prey to Nick's charm (though men are susceptible to it too). He is "a phenomenon, a model of how ideal a man might be" (38). [12]

Seemingly little more of a feminist [13] than Margaret Drabble, for both writers predate the feminist movement, Anita Brookner generally avoids taking us inside the heads of her male characters largely because she concentrates on letting her heroines reveal themselves—and for another reason as well. While she agrees that the greatest heroines (such as Anna Karenina and Emma Bovary) have been created by men (with some of George Eliot's women as possible exceptions), she sees the reason as having to do with a fundamental difference between men and women:

When you start to write a novel you have to learn to internalize your characters, not to describe them from the outside—that doesn't work. [It is a charge that critics often make against her, however.] And this process of internalizing goes on through life. In the case of a male protagonist gradually you begin to internalize him too—if you are lucky—and this is more difficult for a woman and takes longer. Somehow it is more difficult for a woman to get inside a man than for a man to get inside a woman. Men are better at this, let us face it. I think women have an inborn fear of men, which of course they could never confess to. Instinctively they will cower from a man if he shows some kind of energy or violence. So to reconcile your instinct as a woman with a man's instinct takes a long time. A long time. But I'm trying! [14]

In the same interview, however, she admits that she is "finding it surprisingly easy" to get inside the skin of a man.[15] *Look at Me* seems to have been the turning point; although it does not take us inside a male character, it presents virtually Brookner's first sympathetic males (with the exception of Professor Duplessis in *The Debut*), Dr. Simek and the men who admire Mrs. Linton. After it, she writes briefly from the male point of view in *Hotel du Lac* and *The Misalliance;* makes the viewpoints of males equal with those of females in *Family and Friends,* written in between those two novels; and again enlarges her canvas to include males, if not to get directly inside them, in *A Friend from England.*

Critic Nicholas Shrimpton describes Brookner's first novel, *A Start in Life (The Debut),* as the "sort that gives feminist writing a good name."[16] Contrastingly, Annie Roston, in a review of *Look at Me,* expresses the hope that "maybe Anita Brookner's next heroine will have heard about affirmative action."[17] When asked "how it felt to work in the male-dominated atmosphere of Cambridge University in the sixties," Brookner responded as if careless of the tenor of the question: "Nobody looked all that male and I didn't look all that female."[18] She recognizes that feminism has brought mixed results; it has not overcome the distrust between the sexes or made male-female relationships easier but has "enhanced friendship between women," as an interviewer puts it, and relates to the old question of how free any of us can be:

As for feminism, I think it is good for women to earn their living and thereby control their own destinies to some extent. They pay a heavy price for independence though. I marvel at the energy of women who combine husbands, children, and a profession. Anyone who thinks she will fulfill herself in that way can't be realistic. The self-fulfilled woman is far from reality—it is a sort of Shavian fantasy that you can be a complete woman. Besides, a complete woman is probably not a very admirable creature. She is manipulative, uses other people to get her own way, and works within whatever system she is in. The *ideal* woman, on the other hand, is quite different; she lives according to a set of principles and is somehow very rare and always has been. As for the radical feminism of today, the rejection of the male, I find it absurd. It leads to sterility. They say it is a reasoned alternative, but an alternative to what? To continuity?[19]

In fact, many of Brookner's own women, generally minor characters (for example, most of her mothers, including Helen in *The Debut* and Mrs. Pusey in *Hotel du Lac;* Penelope of *Hotel du Lac*), are unsavory, while her heroines are flawed, and she particularly seems to dislike the way even "nice" women (for example, Mrs. Duff in *The Misalliance*) talk about men and treat them like children. Brookner is equally conclusive about many of current formula women's books:

What I can't understand is the radical inauthenticity of some women's novels which are written to a formula: from the peatbogs of Killarney to the penthouses of Manhattan, orgasms all the way! Pornography for ladies. It is not only impure artistically, it is untrue and unfeminine. To remain pure a novel has to cast a moral puzzle. Anything else is mere negotiation.[20]

Chapter Five
Hotel du Lac: "Giv[ing] Herself a Countenance"
A Change of Brooknerian Mood

Thirty-nine-year-old Edith Hope, a writer of romantic fiction (with such names as *The Stone and the Star* and *Le Soleil de Minuit*) under the "more thrusting" (8) pen name Vanessa Wilde, is the star of Brookner's fourth novel, *Hotel du Lac* (1984). She has disgraced herself by jilting Geoffrey Long because of his "mouselike seemliness" (129), the quality ordinarily associated with Pym spinsters and with a person of Miss Hope's own ilk but also because of her *hope*less affair with married David Simmonds. Her friends send her to the hotel of the title to return to her senses. There she works on her next book and encounters foil characters (Mrs. Pusey and her daughter, Jennifer; the Comtesse de Bonneuil; and Monica, with her dog, Kiki) more eccentric or far more worse off than she is. She also receives another proposal, this time for a marriage of convenience with Philip Neville. When she sees her would-be husband coming out of Jennifer's room, she destroys her letter of farewell to David and sends him instead a telegram that says simply that she is "returning."

Essentially Edith remains unchanged, still the romantic. She has acted out the romantic image of herself as looking like Virginia Woolf, has taken a romantic nom de plume, has fallen into bed with David in fantasy fashion, and in the end rejects a safe if duplicitous marriage for the romance of her affair with David. The real problem is the lack of any savory male throughout. David is a waste of her time, though she cannot see his flaws; at the least, she has to choose between flawed alternatives (David and Philip).

Nonetheless, *Hotel du Lac* is refreshing after Brookner's first three novels, particularly after the psychopathology-tinged *Look at Me*. Although many of the same themes and materials are present, here too are humor and wit, introspection and observation without morbidity and emotional vivisection. One can see why the novel won the coveted British Booker-McConnell Prize for 1984.[1] On the one hand, it is as tightly controlled and carefully written as the others; on the other, Brookner seems to have given way to enjoying the writing she is doing, as she actually describes as having happened at some point in her career.[2] Indeed she seems almost to parody—lightly—the first three novels.[3]

The language is a wonderful mix this time, and the wry comments and observations frequently have the this-you-must-remember quality of a Barbara Pym character exclaiming over fox dung's being gray and pointed at both ends.[4] Monica is sure that "the Swiss hate dogs. That's what's wrong with them, if you ask me" (69). Brookner must have become more than a little tired of critics expounding on her ladylike, delicate prose, though the imagery of grayness that pervades the book (even including the blue-gray wedding clothes Edith has chosen) is beautifully evoked at the opening.[5] More description is employed; for example, Edith sees "the green hedgehog shape of a chestnut, split open to reveal the brown gleam of its fruit" (51–52; an image that Brookner uses elsewhere) and keeps before our eyes her "veal-colored" room in the hotel. The language is contemporary without being trendy, tempered by Edith's droll irony, though the snatches of foreign languages (French, bastard French, German) recur, and the reach can be as high as ever: "The here and now, the quotidian, was beginning to acquire substance" (36); Penelope is "accomplished in venery" (57); "It was agreeable to see men, after days in this gyneceum, bringing the place to life" (61); "The beautiful day had within it the seeds of its own fragility: it was the last day of summer" (67); the castle, "dour, grim, a rebarbative silhouette," is "a corrective to the dazzle of the water" (75). Edith, like most of Brookner's other women except the "overdressed" Kitty Maule of *Providence,* Blanche of *The Misalliance,* and perhaps Rachel of *A Friend from England,* is constantly being told that she dresses terribly in her long cardigan, meant to accentuate her resemblance to Virginia Woolf,[6] and her tweed skirt (148) and that she is not bad looking when she puts her mind to it (148). Still, she recognizes some of the chiefs of the world of fashion: "Gucci and Hermès, Chanel and Jean Muir, The White House and Old England" (109). She knows that she has "failed to scale the heights of consumerism that were apparently as open to her as they were to anyone else" (44). She also can juxtapose the dated and the contemporary: "I cannot think or act or speak or write or even dream with any kind of energy in the absence of love. I feel excluded from the living world. I become cold, fish-like, immobile. I implode" (98). Philip Neville is the first Brookner male to have his way with words, and he is as cynical about them as about everything else: "I don't perceive you [Edith] as a distracted being. I mean that if I were younger and more trendy I should probably say that I could deconstruct the signifiers of your discourse" (76). The effective mixture of language is nowhere better displayed than in Edith's description of the mold into which she is cast: "They thought of her as an old maid, or at least a maiden lady. Randy spinsters of her acquaintance turned their eyes heavenward in despair when she answered, no, there was no one in her life, and never guessed that she lied" (85). Jennifer has a "bottom like a large Victoria plum" (18). Monica is "so beautiful, so thin, so over-bred. Her pelvis is like a wishbone!" (80). Perrier water always gives Edith wind (26). The Comtesse de Bonneuil has a bulldog face, belches (32), and sits with her legs apart (a standard Brookner measure of aging and old women, including Dorrie in *A Friend from England*), but "the silence in which she spen[ds] her days [is] palpable" (77). Monica may look like a sphinx (71) to Edith, but she sounds like something out of *Alice in Wonderland* to the rest of us: "a tall woman, of extraordinary slenderness . . . with the narrow nodding head of a grebe" and a "boneless uncoiling movement" (16). Kiwi fruit slips unnoticed off a fork (27). Mrs. Pusey and Monica use Edith "as a buffer state," subjecting her "to a certain amount of balkanization" (79).

Irony is as strong in language here as in situations throughout the Brookner canon. When Edith leaves Geoffrey literally waiting at the altar in one of the great comic reverses of literature and one entirely germane to the Brookner world of women endlessly lamenting their single lot, she has to listen to harangues from her women acquaintances that include such crimes as her "moral turpitude, her childishness, her lack of dignity, trust, loyalty, and decent feminine sensibility" (132). Mrs. Dempster, the recurrent Brookner domestic, only this time a "dramatic and unpredictable cleaning lady" (58), is so dismayed by Edith's betrayal of both Geoffrey and all of her sex that she quits: "She could not see her way clear, she explained, to coming back. She was funny like that. Sensitive. Edith would have to make other arrangements" (134).

Literary allusions are more prevalent and are cleverly arranged. Edith tells David in a letter that she is "sorry not to have written for the last couple of days but the desert of the Hotel du Lac has begun to blossom like the rose with strange new relationships" (79). She announces to

Mr. Neville, with what she hopes is "Nietzschean directness," her desire for coffee (99). Edith's mother has bequeathed to her daughter "her own cloud of unknowing" (104), an image from the mystics that works with other medieval images and references in the novel—for example, writers as "sycophants at court in the Middle Ages, dwarves, *jongleurs*" (91–92)—and suggests that Edith, like previous Brookner heroines, has an interest in the psychic.[7] Edith and the few other guests at the hotel are no fit audience for the "garden of earthly delights" (an allusion doubtless to Hieronymus Bosch's painting) presented by Mrs. Pusey and her daughter, Jennifer (107). When Edith writes her fifth and supposedly final letter[8] to David telling him that she has decided to marry Philip Neville, she draws on literature for her model: "I know, you see, that whatever you feel for me, or perhaps I should say, once felt for me, I am, as Swann said of Odette, not your type" (180).[9]

Like Frances in *Look at Me,* Edith is not forthcoming about herself but presents a persona: "Perfectly composed, tending her garden, writing, her face closed against pity, sympathy, curiosity, Edith kept silent and yearned for David" (84). She is the first Brookner heroine, however, to attract confidences, and she spends a lot of time quietly absorbing those with which people bombard her. We have no sense that she, like Frances, will gain revenge against the world at large by putting such material in her novels. She does literally have a garden that she loves, though the greengrocer's boy, Terry, tends it for her and loves it with her: "the money seemed to them both a separate issue, hardly connected with the loving work of housekeeping to which they both, in their different ways, applied themselves" (121). They have paleness in common, too, and, when she is leaving for the airport in disgrace, he alone supports her: "Edith had been comforted to see Terry, paler than ever, making his steady way along the pavement with a box full of bedding plants. He had raised his free hand, with his spare key in it, when he saw her, and she had waved back. At least, she thought, the garden will be cared for" (134). The allusion is to Voltaire's *Candide* ("cultivating our garden"), and the real question is whether the garden of her soul will be tended. One of the reasons that she has had second thoughts about Geoffrey Long is that he has replaced the "old spreading creaking wicker chair" she used to sit in in her garden to relax from her writing with a "rather uncomfortable wrought-iron bench,"[10] symbolizing to Edith perhaps the death of her writing, for he does not approve of women working. The rancor against Geoffrey also has to do with his threat to the world she has constructed and in which she is much more

content than earlier Brookner women. From that garden, she is her
most humane in the novel:

> At this time, she knew, her neighbour's child, a child of heartbreaking beauty
> whose happiness and simplicity were already threatened by a crippling speech
> defect,[11] would come out to see if she were there (but she was always there) and
> would slip through the hedge to say goodnight. And Edith would watch her
> wrestling with the words, her thin little body juddering [sic] with the effort to
> unlock them, and she would smile and nod as if the words were perfectly
> intelligible, and would put her hands to the child's jerking head to still it, and
> would whisper, "Good night, my little love. Sleep well." And would kiss the
> child, now calm, and send her off to bed. (121)

The entire remembered scene with Edith's agent, Harold Webb,
while it expands the relation between Ruth Weiss and her publisher[12]
framing The Debut, is a tour de force updating Aesop's legend, "The
Tortoise and the Hare," to provide a raucous disquisition on the battle
of the sexes. It can be excised as a literary gem and yet foreshadows the
questions aplay in the novel (and the entire Brookner canon). Edith
Johanna Hope, for all the meekness of her name, really is as sharp-
tongued as Frances thinks people think her to be in Look at Me. She is
also sharp-witted. When Harold tries to get her to consider writing
"sex for the young woman executive" (26), her responses indicate that
she has long since examined and eschewed that avenue for herself,
leaving "those multi-orgasmic girls with the executive briefcases" to
"go elsewhere. They will be adequately catered for. There are hucksters
in every market place" (28).[13] Nobody has a "life-style," and besides,
women "prefer the old myths, when it comes to the crunch. They want
to believe that they are going to be discovered, looking their best,
behind closed doors, just when they thought that all was lost, by a man
who has battled across continents, abandoning whatever he may have
had in his in-tray, to reclaim them" (27). In her books, the mouselike
girl will continue to get the hero, while the scornful temptress will
retreat. The tortoise wins every time in the lies of fiction; the hare, in
real life:

> "And in any case it is my contention that Aesop was writing for the tortoise
> market. Axiomatically," she cried, her voice rising with enthusiasm. "Hares
> have no time to read. They are too busy winning the game. The propaganda
> goes all the other way, but only because it is the tortoise who is in need of
> consolation. Like the meek who are going to inherit the earth," she added,

with a brief smile. . . . "Of course," said Edith, ladling chips of sugar coloured like bath salts into her coffee, "you could argue that the hare might be
affected by the tortoise lobby's propaganda, might become more prudent,
circumspect, slower, in fact. But the hare is always convinced of his own
superiority; he simply does not recognize the tortoise as a worthy adversary.
That is why the hare wins," she concluded. "In life, I mean. Never in fiction.
At least, not in mine. *The facts of life are too terrible to go into my kind of fiction.*
And my readers certainly do not want them there. You see, Harold, my readers
are essentially virtuous." (27–28; my italics)

Because of her wit and general good nature, Edith can get by with her
comic perversion of literature. Frances Linton in *Look at Me* claims to
write humorously and to do exactly what Edith describes, but we do
not trust her, and we are offended by her plainspokenness, a problem
that Brookner has Rachel Kennedy recognize for her case in *A Friend
from England.*

Edith Hope[ful]

Edith is much more assertive and more drolly acerbic than the previous Brookner women. She has listened, past boredom, to the endless
pronouncements, downright dicta, of particularly Mrs. Pusey, who cele-
brates her seventy-ninth birthday at the hotel and whose life, at least
since marriage, has been an endless shopping spree. As Edith descends to
breakfast one morning, she recites a litany of Puseyisms—for example,
"A woman owes it to herself to have pretty things. And if she feels good
she looks good" (43)—but still has to steady "herself with a deep breath
before going out into the world." Her parting shot, however, is double-
edged. "Of course, I have everything delivered" mimics Mrs. Pusey. It
also attests to Edith's recognition that, as a person and a writer, she tends
to take material from others and throw up a persona; she lets others
believe that she has failed to develop a personality and to have experiences
of her own. Again, after watching the prodigious appetites of the Puseys
through four courses, Edith uses a food cliché to skewer them: "Then,
like many greedy women, they sat back fastidiously, as if the food had
scarcely come to their notice. Butter wouldn't melt, thought Edith"
(34). She gets back her own in other quarters as well. Penelope thinks
that her life is the stuff of novels and cannot understand why Edith has
never put her in a book. The sub-rosa response is, "I have, thought
Edith. You did not recognize yourself" (127).

By the time of this fourth novel, Anita Brookner was also probably tired of being compared with Margaret Drabble and Barbara Pym.[14] As she has a habit of drawing attention to devices and techniques utilized in her works (for example, foils), she seems in *Hotel du Lac* to give critics fodder for their mills by deliberately baiting them with Drabble and Pym. The former, for example, will often have her protagonists make the inductive leap of "two hearts beating as one" by having the men in question use the same phrases or think the same thoughts. Brookner, in a rare switching of point of view to a male and a rare change of focus from Edith, has Phillip Neville probe to himself what on earth Edith is doing at the Hotel du Lac just as she asks him the same question about himself (92). The novel also probes the question that hovers in all of Brookner's, Drabble's, and Pym's novels (the behavior most becoming to a woman, particularly in today's mixed-up world) and delineates more "excellent women" (88, 101), a category and nomenclature straight from Barbara Pym, who not only used it for the title of a novel but as the chief type throughout her works.

Brookner seems to make more effective use of her expertise in art history in this novel. In addition to the reference to Delacroix (56), she draws an analogy between Edith's relation to the world and painting: "I rather thought I was useful as an audience, but only as a lay figure is useful to a painter: both can be put aside when no longer required" (76). Ironically, David auctions paintings, among other goods from country estates. Edith hears him announce "Lot Five. *Time Revealing Truth.* Attributed to Francesco Furini. What am I bid?" (88). Shakespeare can comment negatively on a character by having him or her dislike music (and the title of Edith's novel-in-progress, *Beneath the Visiting Moon,* comes from Shakespeare's Cleopatra), and we wonder if David's business association with art should not be a further warning to Edith. The title of the painting is functional, of course, though we can never be certain that the truth about David is revealed to Edith. Again a memory of painting seems to be trying to convey truth to Edith not only about Philip Neville, with whom she is on a lake excursion, but about her life in general:

Somewhere behind the veils of mist there was a pale sun which could be seen, in the far distance, to cast a white gleam on the water. They were to land at Ouchy, where they would lunch, and to come back in the afternoon. But it seemed to Edith that this journey was too serious to be thought of simply in terms of diversion. The empty lake, the fitful light, the dream-like slowness with which they were covering the distance, seemed to have an allegorical significance. Ships, she knew, were often used by painters as symbols of the soul, sometimes of the soul departing for unknown shores. Of death, in fact. Or, if not of death, not of anything very hopeful. Ship of fools, slave ship, shipwreck, storm at sea: such representations, even if not expert, working on that fear that lies dormant even in the strongest heart, upset the nerves and the balance, for such was their intention. Edith, once again, felt unsafe, distressed, unhoused. (159–60)

Following the exceedingly heavy plodding after what writing and the writer are in *Look at Me,* Edith's (and Brookner's) tongue-in-cheek exploration of those topics here is a welcomed change. Edith has the ability to poke fun at herself that is so unfortunately missing from the makeup of Frances Hinton and other Brooknerians. People think that writers absorb every detail (10); Edith does not. The man she meets on the plane must specialize in tropical diseases; actually he has "something to do with tungsten. So much for the novelist's famed powers of imagination" (11). Penelope takes the standard line that "Edith only wrote about those pleasures that reality had denied her" (57), and Edith does admit that, after writing, she is "highly charged with vicarious emotion" (52), the main reason she needs her garden tranquility to unwind.

Edith as a character is simply more appealing than other Brookner women. She presents herself in the same old washed-out, unexciting Brookner heroine way:

I am a householder, a ratepayer, a good plain cook, and a deliverer of typescripts well before the deadline; I sign anything that is put in front of me; I never telephone my publisher [in contrast to Ruth Weiss of *The Debut*]; and I make no claims for my particular sort of writing, although I understand that it is doing quite well. I have held this rather dim and trusting personality together for a considerable length of time, and although I have certainly bored others I was not to be allowed to bore myself. (9)

We are likely to read over that last as, at worst, a dangler; obviously, we think, Edith means that she must entertain and not bore others. But then we read on into the novel, and she becomes revealed as complex enough—and sly enough—to mean what she says: that she will not allow herself to be bored. Actually she seems quite content with the life she has carved—the surface one of fulfilling the expectations of others with regard to the stereotype she cuts as a spinster writer and the inner

one of no small satisfaction to herself. Far more than most of us, she
exacts from those around her the image of herself that she wants them
to have to the point, for example, that she resents Geoffrey's trying to
change her narrow virgin's cotlike affair ("white and plain and not quite
big enough" [122]) for a larger-than-life nuptial bed. (He is not named
"Long" for nothing!) Her first revenge is to let Penelope turn the master
bedroom into something quite alien to Edith and her style:

. . . a counterpane of dull marigold, with expensive marigold coloured tow-
els to hang in their dark green marble bathroom, and some thick satin-bound
blankets the colour of cinnamon. They were new and handsome, but it seemed
to her that they absorbed the light and were stuffily authoritative. She could
not see herself ever repairing to this bedroom after a day's writing, or taking a
nap on the splendid cane-headed bed. And she had noticed precious few
children in Montagu Square, and there was no garden, so that her day would
have an entirely different pattern when her writing time was over. (123)

Her great revenge, of course, is not marrying Geoffrey at all. She can
dismiss him for his "mouse-like seemliness" (129) precisely because she
lets others so dismiss her. Mrs. Pusey invites Edith to join her daughter
and her in the first place because of her "sad eyes" (35). We learn
indirectly that she dreams (like Ruth in *The Debut*, Kitty in *Providence*,
Blanche in *The Misalliance*, and Rachel in *A Friend from England*) because her walk along the lake shore reminds her of "those silent walks
one takes in dreams" (21) and then because, later, "Between disjointed
dreams there flashed onto the cinema screen in Edith's head short
audio-visual messages which she would later have to decode" (64).
Sometimes she cannot tell the difference between dream and reality,
though recognizing that "everything seemed vivid, potent with significance. But the significance was hidden" (65). In such a state, she again
hears that door close. She would like to have a gin and tonic but refrains
not because she would be embarrassed to enter the bar alone but because, in general, "meals in public [are] not to her taste, even when she
[is] accompanied" (25), though, in the café, she takes out a notebook
"to give herself a countenance" (45).
    Unfortunately Edith Hope is just as "hopeless" about the man who
enables her to maintain a secret love life. She knows fully well that the
only person who will bother to get in touch with her while she is in
Switzerland is her agent (29). She knows that David (who has the red
hair in this novel) is "a man who could not deny himself anything. And

that she had a part in his self-indulgence" (86). She cooks for him as his wife will not and knows when he will go to bed with his wife (86) and when he is ready to leave her. She knows that she is not David's type and that his friends suspect him of having affairs but "with a succession of tough young secretaries [preparation for Mousie in *The Misalliance,* as is, perhaps, Geoffrey's "*mouse*-like seemliness"], or with other men's wives" (85), not with someone like her. He drops hints about their affair to his wife and his friends. Again, she can live underneath her public image and likes to do so more for the enjoyment of the game than for being forced to, as other Brookner women tend to be. She may even feel superior to David, as to others, in not needing to reveal herself and her secret ways. We still have to wonder how she can love a man she persists in describing as "foxy" (59) and one who is oblivious of her "empty Sundays, the long eventless evenings, the holidays cancelled at the last minute" (61), that lament of so many other Brookner (and Pym) women. For that matter, how can she take seriously a coming together that is straight out of pulp romantic fiction? They met when she heard a voice say at one of Penelope's parties, "I must be getting back to the Rooms" (56). "Filled with [a responsive] vision of the hammam, the Arab café, the Mediterranean siesta," she asks him to describe "these Rooms." He looks down his long nose and does so. "Then she looked up at him and they exchanged a level glance from which all expression was studiously absent. She lowered her eyes, and he left. Nothing more was said" (59). He comes to her a few hours later, "as she knew he would," and "they said nothing but looked at each other long and hard. In bed, they fell instantly into a warm mutual sleep, arms around each other, and when they woke, almost simultaneously, they had laughed with pleasure. After that, it seemed as if she knew everything about him; the only revelation was his delight-ful and constant appetite" (60–61).

The most interesting male in the novel is Philip Neville, and he is interesting despite his also being cut from a literary pattern. Monica thinks that he "looks rather like that portrait of the Duke of Wellington that was stolen from the National Gallery some time ago" (81), and Edith herself finds him a "curiously mythological personage" (160), "what was once called a man of quality" (97). What is most interesting about him, however, is the animosity he arouses in Edith, who actually at one point shouts that she hates him. The reason may well be that he moves in more closely on the real Edith than anyone else has been able to. In offering her a marriage in name only, he throws into relief the

simulacrum of the world in which she has chosen to live. When she
defies his cynical view that people can live without love, she throws up
her own image of happiness, one that is precisely not what she will get
by returning to her affair with David.

One of the unusual features of this novel is that, in addition to
having women foils to help her make her way—if she would but use
them, either negatively or positively, that is, take the good and eschew
the bad—Edith has men to choose among. If she were the mousy type
people think her and wanted to marry just to be married, she could
settle down and live happily ever after with Geoffrey, even if he has
spent his life heretofore with his mother (as many Brookner and Pym
men seem to do). If marrying to be married mattered that much to her,
she could accept Philip's offer and have even more position and wealth.
She claims, of course, that love means too much to her to accept either
one and apparently means to return to David and settle for love without
the trappings. Brookner admits to having second thoughts about her
heroine's choice: "As I wrote it I felt very sorry for her and at the same
time very angry: she should have married one of them—they were
interchangeable anyway—and at least gain some worldly success, some
social respectability. I have a good mind to let her do it in some other
novel and see how she will cope!"[15]

Hotel du Lac is different too in lacking a good model for Edith,
though the foils provided are exquisite miniature portraits, particularly
the one, again (remembering Maman Louise in *Providence*), of old age.
The Comtesse de Bonneuil, a widow, has presumably had a good
enough marriage, but her son cannot or will not break her loneliness
now. He has married a fortune hunter (a former hairdresser), who has
turned her mother-in-law out of her beautiful home and ensconced her
in the hotel as a perpetual paying guest. She is now old and deaf, and
her life has come down to waiting for the monthly visit of her son, his
wife in impatient tow, dressed in a red dress and spike-heeled sandals.

Monica, something of a fortune hunter herself, has married into a
noble family, though she scorns its members as "jumped-up iron-
mongers" (81), but is also here in exile to try to put herself in order.
Her husband, Sir John, wants and needs an heir, but she suffers from
"an eating problem" (80),[16] feeds her food to her dog, and surrepti-
tiously eats cake at every opportunity ("as others might go slumming"
[80]). She longs for a child and probably will never be able to have one;
thus she will be divorced. Brookner women like to imagine the futures
of others, women and men, and Edith takes Monica's measure:

She hates and fears her husband, but only because he has not protected her, and she sees herself condemned to loneliness and exile. In this she is prescient. I see her, some years hence, a remittance woman, paid to live abroad, in such an hotel, in various Hotels du Lac, her beautiful face grown gaunt and scornful, her dog permanently under her arm. Her last weapon will be an unyielding snobbishness, which is already in evidence. (81)

All of Edith's women foils have some connection with children, none of them happy or salutary. Iris Pusey continues to treat her thirty-nine-year-old daughter as if she were a child while having set Jennifer an example of salaciousness that continues even now when Iris is almost eighty and still sports a luxurious negligée. Their style is self-indulgence; their suite, Aladdin's cave (44), and Jennifer dresses in pink[17] harem pants and looks the odalisque (78), though Edith is still shocked by her affair with Philip. Mrs. Pusey never mentions her husband by name but talks only about his worshiping her (as all women should be worshiped by their husbands [74]; also an issue in *Look at Me*, where it is centered on Frances's mother and father) and providing lavishly for her, and Edith is uncomfortable because her own father has been similarly mistreated by her mother and because the guides for living laid down by Mrs. Pusey are entirely selfish. The "sybaritic" life (45) the Puseys lead embarrasses Edith, who expresses much dissatisfaction with the general run of women she meets. Whether married, they seem to be obsessed by their sexuality as a trap for the male, for whom they have little respect. With such types before us, we see why Edith prefers the company of men.

Much more so than in the first three novels, the protagonist also has her parents as foils. Her father is the most positive portrait in the novel. Mrs. Hope, on the other hand, is somewhat akin to Iris Pusey, though her affection for and attachment to her daughter have nothing in common with the relationship between Edith and her mother. Rosa (Hope) and Anna have been the somewhat infamous "Schaffner sisters," the Viennese "flirts" (48) who represent (with Mme Wienawska, the Polish woman who makes Edith's wedding attire) the foreign element that Brookner likes to introduce among her characters, perhaps in memory of her Polish family. They caught husbands among the students who lodged in their home and are promptly disappointed, for their husbands, "so attractive away from home, turned all too soon into mild university men" (48) and became "too puny to interest them" (49). Edith's mother is a "harsh disappointed woman, that former beauty who raged so unsuccessfully against her fate, deliberately, willfully letting herself go, slatternly and scornful, mocking her pale silent daughter who slipped so modestly in and out of her aromatic bedroom, bringing the cups of coffee which her mother deliberately spilled" (48). What Edith has learned has come from her father (150). He has taught her to remember that "character tells" in times of difficulty (30) and not to make quick judgments. Thus, having condemned women so frequently in the novel, she recognizes that she must not judge all of them by her mother's model: "Edith, Father would have said, think a little. You have made a false equation" (88). She has also betrayed another model: "I have taken the name of Virginia Woolf in vain, she thought" (88). In spite of all, too, her father used to call her mother "my dear life" (12).

The Novel as Novel

Not only is *Hotel du Lac* more enjoyable reading as a story than the first three novels; it is exceedingly well written. It mingles a third- and first-person point of view, both Edith's, with an occasional abrupt shift to the thoughts of men. In one of these sudden shifts, Harold Webb confirms her Virginia Woolf looks (27), and Philip sees her face lose "its habitual faintly sheeplike expression, its quest for approval or understanding" and "become amused, patrician" (92). It uses a variety of approaches as well—for example, some four letters that Edith writes to David summarizing and "editing" what has happened at the Hotel du Lac, reminiscence, and description.

While still a novel of characters and of manners, *Hotel du Lac* has suspense and much more in the way of a plot. The suspense is manipulated along two lines. First, we know that Edith Hope has been sent into exile in Switzerland to regroup and come to her senses after some sort of great faux pas, but the nature of her crime is withheld until the opening of chapter 9 when she, startlingly, begins to tell us about her wedding day and leaving Geoffrey and their friends waiting in the Registry Office. We have been led to believe that we have another never-get-a-man woman, particularly since she is thirty-nine. Second, Brookner builds suspense by having Edith vaguely conscious of hearing a hotel door close at odd hours and by incrementally building episodically to the ultimate scene that functions as another vignette or epiphany bringing revelation and action (like those in *Providence* and *Look at Me*). The first clamor derives from Philip Neville's supposedly having been called to dispose of a spider in Jennifer's room. The second has Mrs. Pusey accuse Alain (the hotel porter) of trying to accost her daughter and will cost him his job. Neither these two episodes, with Philip at hand, nor the mysterious sounds of the doors closing at odd hours prepare Edith for the sight of Philip's emerging from Jennifer's bedroom at the moment when she is on her way to mail a letter informing David that she will marry the man.

Hotel du Lac is a daring novel in which Brookner calls attention to the difference between her kind of writing and Edith's romance novels in the vein of Barbara Cartland and of Mills and Boon. In case we have missed the distinction—and many of the novel's critics did miss it— she has also developed the difference along critical lines:

Romance novels are formula novels. I have read some and they seem to be writing about a different species. The true Romantic novel is about delayed happiness, and the pilgrimage you go through to get that imagined happiness. In the genuine Romantic novel there is confrontation with truth and in the "romance" novel a similar confrontation with a surrogate, plastic version of the truth. Romantic writers are characterized by absolute longing—perhaps for something that is not there and cannot be there. And they go along with all the hurt and embarrassment of identifying the real thing and wanting it. In that sense Edith Hope is not a twentieth century heroine, she belongs to the nineteenth century.[18]

Chapter Six
Family and Friends: "Lavender and Vetiver and 'the Advantage of Rules and Regulations' "

Enlarging the Canvas

Brookner enlarges both canvas and range of techniques in *Family and Friends* (1985), her fifth novel, whose focus is on the Dorns, their individual portraits presented through commentary on a series of family photographs. Full-blown examinations emerge here of the matriarch, Sofka; her charming and inconsequential older son, Frederick; her hardworking, disciplined, and unhappy younger son, Alfred; her virtuous older daughter, Mimi; and her bohemian, breakaway younger daughter, Betty. Minor portraits include those of Lautner (the devoted majordomo of the family business) and the domineering domestic, Muriel. Only infrequently and glancingly before has Brookner entered the consciousnesses of men (Edith's agent and Mr. Neville in *Hotel du Lac*), though she has given slight and external views of sympathetic males (Professor Duplessis in *The Debut*, Dr. Simek and the men who admire Mrs. Linton in *Look at Me,* and Edith's father in *Hotel du Lac*). In the other novels, Brookner distinguishes two classes of women: the "excellent" or good and those of *mauvais genre*, who get their ways by strident self-forcefulness. Here she subsumes in the self-divided Alfred what she depicts as the two principal human (rather than female) categories: "on the one hand a figure embodying loyalty, piety, constraint, and on the other the irresistible lineaments of subversion." This book also brings to a fine point the theme of the others: "the good live unhappily ever after" (as well as including other examples of Brookner's unusual attentiveness to redheads); however, the unprincipled (represented most fully in Betty) do not manage to find the lives they have wanted either. The prodigals (Frederick and Betty) nonetheless remain their mother's favorites. The power of the mother figure, evident in most of Brookner's other novels, would seem to get full play here. Ironically Sofka loses control of her stage-managed children while retaining their affection. Another recurrent Brookner theme in *Family and Friends* is the damage that can be done by letting literature direct life, as is the case with Alfred.

The character who has most in common with Brookner's usual focus is Mimi. Her life is tainted by the failure of a romantic fantasy that Frank, the lover of her sister, will come to her in her Paris hotel room. She languishes and does good works until, at age thirty-five, she is persuaded by her mother to marry old Lautner, have a child, and become "a real woman at last" (134). Instead her mother dies, and she loses the child and assumes the role of the matriarch herself.

Brookner's Most Fully Drawn Mother Figure

Offstage or onstage, mothers usually exert a powerful and negative influence on the heroines—on all of the children in *Family and Friends*—and a problem in this novel is Brookner's change in tone toward the matriarch, Sofka (Sophie) Dorn. She is trenchantly surveyed in the first-person examination of the initial family portrait opening the novel and hoisted on her own and the stereotypical petard of misshaping the lives of her children from the onset, only to become an object of our pity before the book is through. Finally, everyone, as is customary in Brookner's world, ends, if not tragically, then at least trapped in a diminished world. Again we have the strong impression that the author is expressing her ambivalence toward her own Old World ambience.

Sofka's is a fuller portrait of the mother figure than we have had from Brookner's pen. She left her family behind, never seeing even her parents again, to marry a true ladies' man, whose success in business seems directly related to the figure he cuts. He was "easily bored" by his young wife's "inflexible dignity" and died "mildly disgraced. Gambling, they say" (8). Everyone, especially Sofka, is aware of what a catch he was. She knows, as so many other Brookner people know, that personal beauty bestows a license for unconventional and selfish behavior,[1] and she simply blesses her stars that her husband has been discreet about the affairs to which he was thus entitled. She can be glad that he died young and so avoided the loss of his looks and vigor. A special touch in developing Sofka's own portrait is a subtle revealing of the woman's erotic memories of her husband when she finds her daughter Betty trying on the nightgown Sofka bought for a special holiday trip:

Not only has Betty taken it out of Sofka's chest of drawers; she is peering at the piquant little body which it reveals, well aware that she is more finely made than her mother. Sofka and Betty both see this at the same time. And that nightgown has not been worn since Sofka's husband, the reprobate, died. The conjunction of all these reflections has given Sofka a sense of grievance which is periodically mobilized into a headache, for nothing on this earth would permit Sofka to brood on certain aspects of her long and respectable widowhood. (37)

Our initial impression is harsh. The narrator-viewer questions whether the photograph is a wedding portrait, for the bride and groom are displaced from attention by the imperious Sofka. No one seems to have as much right as she to be in this family portrait: "It is as if she has given birth to the entire brood, but having done so, thinks little of them. This I know to be the case. She gazes out of the photograph, beyond the solicitations of the photographer, her eyes remote and unsmiling, as if contemplating some unique destiny. Compared with her timeless expression, her daughters' pleading smiles already foretell their future" (8). We are led to believe that the future to be opened to us has already been molded for the children by their mother. We can already see that "handsome Frederick" will "engage his mother's collusion in many an amorous escapade" but will end a disappointment (8). We can already see Alfred's eyes "shadowed with the strain of behaving well" (8). Sofka, believing that the futures of her children will be shaped by how they are called, has "named her sons after kings and emperors and her daughters [Mireille/Mimi and Babette/Betty] as if they were characters in a musical comedy" (10). Betty will later outdo her mother in this regard by assuming the name "Bunny" when she tries to become a dancer in the Moulin Rouge.

The boys are to conquer; the girls, to flirt (10). Sofka only momentarily indulges Frederick in his violin playing and Alfred in his reading. When the time comes, they will both become "tycoons" and "captains of industry" and face up to their responsibilities to revitalize the factories and the family (10). In the meantime, Sofka has made the boys in her own image while simultaneously encouraging prodigal Frederick the "boulevardier," the "frequenter of the streets," to break hearts and be admired, like his father, as "a man with a bad reputation" (11) with regard to women. They will marry women carefully selected by Sofka for them on the basis not of looks but of similar background and temperament to herself.

The two girls are meant to long to become "virtuous young matrons" practiced in good housewifery, also in the pattern of their mother. In the meantime, they will occupy themselves with innocent flirting and breaking of hearts, never to know "hopeless or unrequited passion and . . . spared the shame of being left unclaimed" (13). Looking at them, Sofka does have some fears for their innocence in this world. She, of course, cannot finally determine their destinies, as the narrator suggests when Sofka looks into the garden and sees a wheelbarrow that has not been put away: "She frowns slightly. How tiresome that so innocent a detail should spoil the perfect picture of her day" (18). Similarly, none of her children turns out as she has orchestrated, though all remain aware of the dangers (and attractions) of falling into what Sofka calls *mauvais genre* (e.g., 91, 155) or "bad form."

Sofka is a kindhearted woman. When her former friend from the old country, Irma Beck, having fallen on bad times as a result of the war, unwittingly arrives at the door of her new flat in Bryanston Square to sell lace, Sofka not only brings her inside but has Lautner provide funds for her, and Lautner later arranges for Irma's son, George, to be taken into Dorn and Company. Sofka gives jobs to displaced Lili and Ursie, treats them as part of the family, and will see that they have dowries. They appear in the final portrait in the book, and a marriage is in the offing for George Beck and Ursie. Again Brookner gives Sofka's motives an ironic edge, for "Lili and Ursie, harsh hectic girls with unpredictable moods and extravagant loving impulses, have long fulfilled some emotional need of Sofka's; they serve in a sense to replace those children of hers who have gone, and they supplement, in some vital way, the excellent qualities of those children who remain" (100). Sofka knows that the worst and the "most interesting" of her children have disappeared (101), Betty to America and Frederick to the Hotel Windsor in Italy. Worse, she has sentenced Alfred to a life against his grain, by the power of his affection for her, when her favorite, Frederick, proves to be good only at the pampered life for which she has fitted him and in which she encourages him. When she suddenly finds that Alfred may break away too, and in the most unpleasant way—running off with his married cousin, Dolly— she arranges for Lautner, in effect an old family retainer, to marry Mimi. With Mimi gone, Alfred will not be able to leave Sofka on her own. When she sees her younger son becoming like his father, Sofka is pinioned by her creator's simile. She "addresses the Almighty, rather as she would address her bank manager":

I have loved them [her children], she assures the deity in whom she does not
fully believe. I think they have loved me. I am tired now. All I ask is that I
should keep them a little longer. There will be time later. If Alfred is to make
a fool of himself, at least let him avoid bringing disgrace on the family. You
know that I have done my best. I have kept the faith. Please let Alfred settle
for an *affaire* rather than insist on a divorce. That is what my husband always
did, and everybody seemed to like him for it. I really do not understand these
matters. Please let Alfred stay with me. If I am to lose anyone, let it not be
Alfred. The best solution would be for Mimi to find a good man and marry
him. Alfred would not then leave me alone. You know that I am getting old. I
do not know how long I have left. I have not asked for much, but all in all I
have been grateful. I only ask for Alfred's sake. He has always been so good.
And it would be a pity if he were to change. (123)

The pain she feels for the suffering Mimi is tinged with resentment
that, still at home and unmarried, this daughter continues to trouble
her mother (106). *Family and Friends* is also very much a study in the
awful tyranny of the parent.

Sofka uses the truth as she and her generation know it against Mimi,
withholding only her own fear of being left alone. She calls Mimi to
attention with a loud and "archaic" use of the word *daughter* and to
account with this fearful canvas:

I do not want to die and leave you alone. I do not want you to remain my
little child, without your mother to run to. Do you know what they say of
such women? Do you know what it is like for a woman to grow old without a man? To be a godmother to other women's children, useful for presents and otherwise disregarded? Do you know what it is like never to set a
family table? Never to celebrate? To sit alone, because it is inconvenient for
your friends to invite you? Do you know what it is to be left out of other
people's plans? To be left out of their conversations, even? Do you want to
grow old like this, playing the piano, dreaming like a girl? Do you know
the names that other women apply to women like you? . . . They talk
about you. As if you had some fatal illness, which God forbid. But they
will not talk about you after your wedding. Lautner is not undignified. He
is a good man. And no one will talk about you in that way when they see
your house, when they admire your possessions, when they come to your
afternoons. Papa left you a settlement, you know. You will not be poor.
And when you have a child of your own, then you will no longer be angry
with your mother. Then, my darling, you will rejoice and be proud and be
a real woman at last. (133–34)

The description is not exaggerated for the old-fashioned world to which Sofka clings. It merely leaves out one of her motivations: her own fear of being left alone.

Strangely, for the first time in her life, after she agrees to marry Lautner, Mimi does not defer to Alfred and to others. The very act of marrying pulls her from her state of sleepwalking through life, though to a man not intended for her: "For she knows, instinctively, that she was meant to be the wife of a man so inevitably, so truly loved that he would *validate* [again that principal desire of the standard Brookner woman] her entire existence. And that without such a love she will remain *invalid,* insignificant, and, worse, disabused" (132; my italics). Mimi Lautner may give in to the image of marriage painted by her mother, but she is, ironically, infinitely more viable than the quiescent Mimi Dorn who mourns and blames the absence of a quality in herself for preventing Frank (Franko) Cariani from coming to claim her in that Parisian hotel room so many years back, as Kitty Maule in *Providence* has blamed her own inadequacies for her not being able to entice Maurice Bishop. In her wedding portrait, Mimi looks "extremely gracious, rather grand" also for the first time in her life. She has surprised them all by "wearing white peau-de-soie and carrying a great many flowers" (137).

The problem with the portrait of Sofka is the lack of recognition that she, too, is trapped by her Old World upbringing and view, as other characters in Brookner are trapped by the worldview they absorb from literature and folk legacy (for example, Alfred in this book by the world of Dickens, Brookner women generally by the story of Cinderella). Thus she cannot see—and there is no reason why she should be able to see—a middle way between dignity-virtue and license. Sofka is victimized by her own culture, though we may feel that Brookner refuses to recognize her helplessness to be otherwise. She sees only that "possession of a husband confers status on a woman" and "that a woman of thirty-five [Mimi] without a husband is to be pitied, and is indeed pitied by those who ignore her essence and who will almost certainly denigrate her virtues" (125). Her beliefs have been conferred, too, by the Bible, and she herself is the apotheosis of its virtuous woman whose price is above that of rubies. These mainstreams of thought and culture constantly inform Brookner's characters that they should expect to become apotheoses of various virtues. By such standards of measurement, Sofka can overlook what she does to Mimi and Alfred. The parable of the prodigal son tells her that it is all right for the profligates among her children, Frederick and Betty, to be her favorites.

The Men

In *Family and Friends,* for the first time, we have full-blown portraits of men, the brothers Frederick and Alfred, with glimpses of Lautner and the general class of men who marry women connected with the Dorn family. As is the case with Margaret Drabble, we quickly see that men and women in the Brookner world have much in common. They tend to be either herbivores or predators (the classes established in Drabble's first novel, *A Summer Bird-Cage*), givers or takers, the restrained or the willful. Most of them are the first in each continuum and want to be their opposite. In spite of the belief of the majority— "that the good live unhappily ever after" (183)—few Brookner people, male or female, are happy.

The artistic coup in *Family and Friends* is that the brothers, Alfred the good and Frederick the profligate, offer such variation on their individual types and at the same time are united through a relationship with their mother tinged with sexual overtones and paralleling the father-daughter entanglements of other Brookner novels (and reflected in Mimi here). In actuality, each brother turns out to upend the type he portrays. Frederick appears to have been molded by his mother to spend a lifetime in the "nonchalant stance of the Apollo Belvedere" (17) watching the women who watch him but perpetually engaged in a pseudo-courtship of his mother, Sofka, and in league with her against all other women who pursue him; "somehow, out of the unpromising debris of a European family, Sofka has bred an English aristocrat" (22). Entirely unreliable, Frederick dismisses his shortcomings as failures of memory and those ladies who upbraid him as neurotics (and is joined in this dissection by other women [20]). He cannot abide complaints and unpleasantness from anyone but most especially from that other sex. Sofka dismisses his failures as the legacy of "his father's legendary way with women" (20). She lies for him, waits up to receive his confidences, and welcomes his girlfriends at tea on Sundays. Ultimately giving up on him, his suitors—he is courted rather than doing the courting— marry, and he visits and remains their friend. They learn to make his favorite, marzipan cake, and their husbands are glad to have him as a *Hausfreund,* a wife's companion. If Alfred feels neutered by his goodness, Frederick the voluptuary appears to be neutered in the eyes of the husbands of his former girlfriends. He is too lazy and spoiled, they feel, "to do much more than make intimate conversation" (27). They watch him grow plump: "He is now violin shaped [where he once played the violin], and his beautiful face has the ruined charm of a professional voluptuary" (30). Sofka has never wanted her children to marry too young, but, in the case of Frederick, she has encouraged his life-style too long. When his laziness prevents his seeing that Betty actually takes the train from France to Switzerland and she breaks away for a life of her own, he loses ground with his mother, who finds that he is not to be relied upon in matters vital to the family. In business, Frederick, who should run his father's factory, is unable to treat work in any way other than as play. The original *homo ludens,* he may get to work in the afternoon or not at all but remains a favorite with those who work in the factory and those who are its customers, though all the work is done by Lautner and, later, by his brother, Alfred.

Evie, the woman who gets Frederick, possesses what most other Brookner people, including Mimi in this novel, long for: a self-forcefulness, *l'élan vital,* that seems to partake of the life force itself: "it is as a member of the species, in those days before the lava cooled, that she is most *viable.* That is Evie's trump card: *viability*" (73; my italics). She pits her animal vitality and her sexual power against Sofka's promotion of charm and wins. Again Sofka's program for one of her children has failed. In fact, Frederick has become feminine: "He adores women, he appreciates them, he maddens them with his knowledge of their little ploys. He bathes in an entirely feminine atmosphere, and in this way subtly eludes that English persona that his mother has decreed for him and reverts to more distant origins. The violin player in the provincial coffee-house was not altogether wide of the mark" (74; an image used for him earlier). In his marriage, he will play the feminine role; Evie, the masculine (e.g., 76). The subverting "man of the world" has been, ironically, subverted, another case in this novel of one being "hoist[ed] with his own petard." Sofka's inculcation of social gamesmanship has made Frederick effete and bored: "All those years of half-measures, of flattery and *badinage,* of conquests too easy because they were largely unsought, have dulled his appetite for dainty fare. He now seeks cataclysms and no longer cares for disguise" (75). Evie obliges and easily enslaves him as Brookner shows in one of her infrequent highly and thoroughly erotic images: "Evie has only to throw back her head in a peal of laughter, revealing her trembling pink uvula, than Frederick is subjugated. Never before has he been so closely in touch with the mysteries of the flesh. For Frederick, despite all his winning ways, is a genuine voluptuary" (75–76). Evie will reenslave him as he watches her breastfeeding their twins.

Sofka will never see that the stage-set world she has arranged for her older son has made him a voluptuary in all matters, not just in matters sexual. Evie is wise enough to continue, in the pattern of his mother, to treat Frederick as a guest in his own home—ironically, a hotel in Italy owned by her father where he can play the genial host to all who come near, including the Germans during the war years. This favorite child of Sofka never thinks of going home to her or to England, which has become a mere source of Start-Rite shoes, Dundee marmalade, and Floris's New Mown Hay (which is poured into the late afternoon bath over which he lingers).[2] He does not have to go back; he knows his own trump card. Having fathered twins, he is the only one of Sofka's children to put himself beyond reproach by fulfilling the biblical injunction to go forth and multiply (another excellent example of the way Brookner shows the influence of the lore of the culture). Sybaritic, he is not excessive even so and is merely a masculine version of a type first introduced in Mrs. Pusey of *Hotel du Lac*. Each day he goes to Nice to walk through the marketplace, almost never to make a purchase, though he often imagines participating in the life of the market, for "the place has become essential to him as a storehouse of further sights, smells, and impressions to feed his ever greedy sensorium" (145). He may stop in the Church of St. Rita and light a candle. He will go to the café, speak French with the waiter, and drink espresso but almost never anything more—"For Frederick rarely drinks, and in any case seems to despise any additional stimulus which might heighten and ultimately falsify his own excellent imagination" (146–47). He will spend an hour or so at the gaming tables, neither winning nor losing much. Women remain interested in him, but he denies them gently, still believing that the man offers and the woman gratifies, a view that Evie encourages and the reason that they are pointed out as such a devoted couple. He returns home and spells her for a short time in the evenings before his family gathers for the public dinner that heightens their image as the perfect group, and the never-failing, never-flagging charm of his youth at his mother's is exerted to please the hotel guests. The only flaw in his perfect life is that rediscovery each day that the print of the newspaper has soiled his hands (a clever link with his mother and her upset over the wheelbarrow out of place). He does not even return to England for his mother's funeral. Frederick has "dematerialized into the

Riviera sun" (183), his life one of daily rituals that please the senses—but only lightly and gently. He is not the profligate after all, merely the overrefined. Already his own children "speed about Europe fearlessly on their mopeds and plan to settle in America as soon as they are old enough" (183). *Family and Friends* has no true unprincipled. Nor does any other Brookner novel. All of the canon, however, has someone the other characters think to be in this class.

One critic feels that Frederick's portrait is central: "As the story proceeds, each character's loss of innocence makes him or her affecting; and in their disillusionment, the author captures that of a generation and a culture. Frederick, the old charmer, evokes the most pathos, settling into middle age as a hotel keeper on the Italian Riviera. Faintly ridiculous, 'portly now, but light on his feet, Frederick lifts his hat to ladies young and old in the streets of Bordighera.' "[3] But no pathos resides in the portrait of Frederick. He is the most contented of Sofka's children, and most people would like to be so contented. The irony in his presentation is that he is uncomprehending of what has happened to him: being taken over entirely first by his mother and then his wife and being made in the image they have cast for him. One of the points of the novel is the devious power of such women. The Dorn women, types themselves, easily convert their husbands to types:

I have no doubt that those anonymous and jovial men (husbands, of course) [being viewed by the narrator in one of the family portraits] relaxed into the sweetness of this precarious harmony, having found at last what married life had seemed to promise them, and their golden smiles, their passive decent good natures, the sudden look of worldliness their faces assumed as their lips closed voluptuously round the fine Romeo y Julietas and they lifted their heads a little to expel the bluish smoke reminded their wives—censorious women, with higher standards—why they had married them. (9)

Brookner's almost cruel portraits of the manipulative powers of some of her women, even well-intentioned women, stand in contrast to the repressed, "lonely me" types at the other end of the spectrum. On the other side, the men seldom realize that they are being manipulated or that they themselves repress.

One of the greatest ironies and cleverest efforts of *Family and Friends* is the change in Alfred, subtly revealed in the final family portrait of the book. This younger son has idolized his mother, and she has used that idolatry to transform him, despite his wishes and bent, into the man of business who has rebuilt the family fortunes. Alfred the good and Alfred the reader (his favorite, *The Conquest of Peru*) are destined to compensate for Frederick's "vanished charm with a lifetime of unstinting toil" (28). Sofka knows and has determined that "Frederick is for leisure, for diversion, for entertainment; Alfred is for work, for investment, for security" (49). She may not know, at least fully, that with Alfred, too, her relationship is somewhat sexual, that as she sees him off each morning in her Japanese silk peignoir and prepares his favorite foods for dinner, she is trapping him forever between "two kinds of love: the one that cares for your welfare, your food, your comfort, and the one that engages your wildest dreams and impulses" (47). Only very late will he seek the embodiment of the latter. For now, he is actually repulsed by encounters with it, beginning with the "impurity" of his sister Betty, one of several redheads in this novel:

Alfred's purity reacts instinctively to another's impurity; what he feels for Betty is not in fact hatred but disgust. Alfred senses about Betty, when she passes him, a sharpish odour, the acid sweat of a true redhead, which makes him grit his teeth. In this way, and for this reason, he will always be resistant to the odours of women, shocking them sometimes by a very slight movement of recoil when they bend to kiss him. For this reason too he will only be accessible to a woman whom he recognizes as akin to himself, or to a woman so artificially fragrant that he does not sense her real presence. [The latter is what actually happens: Dolly's overt sexuality is masked by her gardenia scent. What Alfred wants is a Dorrie Livingstone, whose honeysuckle scent in *A Friend from England* declares her the genuine and acceptable (stereotypical) female article.]
    Alfred's heavy burden of feeling, his purity, and his scorn have added a lowering quality to his handsome face which makes him doubly attractive to certain types of women, usually older women. He is perhaps Hippolytus to their Phaedra, and they look at his tall slim body, his long eyelashes, and the compressed line of his red lips and wonder how it would be to initiate him into the mysteries of love . . . [.] Alfred, stern and unbendingly dutiful, inspires these feelings in a whole range of women, from Frederick's motherly secretary to one or two of Sofka's friends. All are careful to censor their reactions, allowing themselves only an anxious smiling concern for his condition. Alfred is preoccupied by his condition and therefore does not notice the range of female sensibilities to which he has access. When he is a little older, this imperviousness will drive women to unwise acts and statements, which they will later regret. (46–47)

Alfred may get almost physically ill at the thought of reporting to the factory, but go he will because his mother insists that the fate of the family rests with him. At sixteen, he is sent, and no one bothers to offset his life of work with the emoluments of riches; he is paid a child's wages and has to purchase a six-volume set of Shakespeare on the installment plan until Mimi buys it for him as a gift. She is also the only one who bothers to knock before entering his room. He will supplant Frederick once and for all as the family manager when he goes to Paris with Mimi to learn what has happened to Betty. Yet it will actually be the sister who finds Betty and deals with her. Alfred will be diminished in an exchange with a cordial salesman on the train (he will always suffer from such personal insecurity) and will spend his time arranging access to the family funds his father has left in the care of their Paris lawyer, Maître Blin. He will insist that he and Mimi eat in their suite, "for Alfred is in fact quite seriously disturbed by the French in their informal mode. He finds them threatening, confident, and much cleverer than he is, and he knows that at the bank they were expecting him to be Frederick" (68). His seventeenth birthday will thus pass unnoticed by the family. It is little wonder that Alfred lacks a pleasing, fetching personality. People at the factory worked harder for the lazy but charismatic Frederick. Alfred dislikes his brother, hates his sister Betty, and takes steps to block Lautner's access to his mother and their home. He is a rather classic example, in the Drabble mode, of a character upon whom strain has taken its toll.

Also Drabbelian about Alfred is his having been shaped by literature (as well as by his mother). Heretofore in Brookner, it is women (often the protagonist) who are so directed and who act out or try to act out literary enjoinings. As a small boy, all Alfred wanted to do was read. What he has gleaned makes him able to endure his life but also promises something unlikely to be delivered unto him anymore than unto all other Brookner protagonists, who believe in reward for living the good life and in ultimate apotheosis as much as he:

Alfred, trying to deal with the antipathy that this way of life has forced upon him, and trying also to deal with the good conscience which is perhaps only blamelessness in disguise and can be forfeited at any moment, knows from his reading that *virtue is its own reward*. This seems to him rather hard, for by the same token vice is also its own reward. But if he translates his predicament into fiction, if he views it as a pilgrimage, or a perilous enterprise or an adventure, if, in fact, he thinks of himself as Henry V or as Nicholas Nickleby [an important influence on Brookner herself], then he can soldier on, comforted by the thought that his efforts and his determination and all his good behaviour will be crowned with success, recognition, *apotheosis*. (50; my italics)

Alfred also wants to enact the stereotypes of life that he has found
largely in his reading. Very un-English in fact, the family, at his
insistence, begins to act out Sunday lunch in the quintessential English
and Dickensian mode with Alfred "flourishing carving knives" and
exerting "his patriarchal will on a large roast of beef" (77) while secretly
wishing for the old days when Frederick sat at the head of the table and
he sat at Sofka's side where "he could turn to her and whisper requests"
(77). (Despite the tyranny Sofka has exerted, all of her children look
back with longing to the days of their childhood in her home.) With
the war, Alfred saw his last hope of escape closed off. "Looking not so
much for a means of serving his country as for an *honourable discharge*
[surely an intended pun] from family matters" (102; my italics), he has
been refused the right to join the army but required to do "essential and
secret work" for it at the factory, though even Sofka does not know what
this task involves. More irritable and unforgiving than ever, he compen-
sates by using his riches and moves the household back to the vacated
opulently masculine flat of an oil man in Bryanston Square, the London
area where he faintly remembers living as a child. Then, drawing still
on his residue of literature, he immediately begins, like Anthony
Keating in Drabble's *The Ice Age* with his High *Rook* House, to search
for the mythical "house in the country"—*Wren* House—that is to resolve his standard Brooknerian feelings of not fitting in, and he is as
beset by dreams as the typical Brookner heroine. With an especially
cruel irony, the golden people of this novel are "golden dogs":[4]

He has visions, largely nourished by reading, of the sort of home he has never
known; this sort of home is bound up with a certain concept of the land, of
rootedness, which is proving strangely elusive. In such a home, thinks Alfred,
he will find his true centre; the aches and sorrows of childhood will disappear
at last, never to return. For they have stayed with him, these sorrows. The
effortfulness of being the model son has never quite disappeared, and the
handsome face and the prosperous habits have never quite replaced the child in
whose good character his mother took such a pride. Sometimes Alfred has a
dream in which he is running through a dark wood; at his heels there are two
beautiful golden dogs, his familiars, and with them he is running through the
dark wood of his pilgrimage towards the golden dawn of his reward. It is this
strange dream that has determined Alfred to look for his real home. (103)

If he finds this "mythical home" (106) and thus completes his "mythic
quest, as it were for the grail" (107), he will have received the sign that
his "efforts have been recognized" (103), and he will be his own man at

last, ready to "consume hecatombs of women, behave as badly as Frederick, care nothing for the feelings of others" (103).[5] Wren House turns out not to be what he really wants, and it comes with an imperious housekeeper who, along with his own restlessness, divides him from his mother for the first time. He will remain dissatisfied: "In what glade, in what grove, can Alfred find his peace?" (110).

Alfred is destined to go through life on the horns of dilemmas because he, like so many other Brooknerians, cannot see middle ways between the extremes of life's continua. He is the principled wishing to be the unprincipled. He believes that he lives a life of conformity and that viability is to be found only in the life of excess. He is determined to stop having others' ways and have his own for once. Having ostensibly found his home, he believes that he "has reached that point in his life when his appetites will be made either risible or entirely valid" (118). The way to validity, ironically, is his scent-laden cousin Dolly, a former conquest of Frederick, who dubbed her the "Lady of the Gardenias" (for the reader, a satirical allusion to Dumas fils' *La Dame aux Camélias*).[6] When, at Wren House, Dolly and Alfred, before her husband, Hal, and the rest of the family, go off alone, the vignette is like a deliberate parody of Henry James (the Baronness de Vionnet and Chad revealed to Lambert Strether once again). His appearance when they return is shocking: "he has lost his composure, his gravity. In their place there is a curious hilarity; he has never looked so young. He has ceased, almost in an instant, to observe the wishes of other people; he has thrown over all his careful upbringing; he is reconciled with the prospect of behaving in dubious taste" (119). When Dolly then cooks scrambled eggs and generally wrests the household from the housekeeper, Muriel, Alfred is so far gone as to see only that, at last, his table begins to resemble those tables he has read about in Dickens and that Dolly behaves like his mother's niece:

It is with the conviction that he has reached a watershed that Alfred allows himself to be so joyous. He has the mistaken impression that all those present both understand and forgive his behaviour. This is by no means the case. This air of family unity serves to disguise the unforgivable facts; for it is as a family that they are united and it is as a family that they will be disunited. The connection between Dolly and Alfred must not be examined: the taboos of the old world [not only adultery but incest since they are cousins] still obtain. And if Alfred, in his new spirit of liberation, and Dolly, in her old spirit of self-regard, are quite comfortable in this atmostphere, there are those present who are not. (121)

Progress in the affair is stalled by the illness of Sofka, who cannot seem to recover from a bout of influenza. The family gathers to await her death and to watch the silent but palpable pulls between Alfred and Dolly. At the point of trying to release himself for a "life of risk and impropriety," he comes most to "resemble a character in classical tragedy or allegorical painting: on the one hand a figure embodying loyalty, piety, constraint, and on the other the irresistible lineaments of subversion" (171). He feels betrayed by Mimi, who has forsaken her mother and her brother for Lautner, and he detests her old husband for getting her pregnant. Inwardly developing "a state bordering on psychopathy," he contemplates showing them all by running off with Dolly and leaving them to their own resources: "he must vindicate his buried self [perhaps a memory of Matthew Arnold's "buried life"], that essential self still burning beneath the lava accretions of duty, foresight, prudence, accountability, reputation, regularity, good manners, and the unvarying performance of the high-principled man of affairs" (172). Yet he recognizes that Dolly is not a "long-term prospect" (173), merely the first to spill from the Pandora's box his commitment to license will open.

As Betty comes to resent her own husband Max's interest in her family, Alfred has resented and resisted Lautner's intrusion. His desire to become part of England notwithstanding, Alfred cannot understand that Lautner ceases to be the outsider for the first time in his life when he marries Mimi and is allowed to call Sofka "Mama." He is the protector of the Old World ways, which Sofka has unwittingly almost bred out of her own children, and recalls Alfred to them at the matriarch's deathbed in a scene considered by one critic as the best in the book and its "poignant and dramatic climax."[7] Sofka's death retraps her son, who, "obeying some ancestral impulse," covers his mother's mirror with a silk shawl, and, stage-managed now by Lautner as formerly by Sofka, falls in with Old World rituals of death: rending his garments and accepting the appropriate biblical passage for Sofka—"A virtuous woman who can find? Her price is above rubies" (178). Standing all night in her room, he admits, "I never meant to leave you . . . and now knows it to be true" (178). All thought of running away with Dolly dies with his mother. Instead he sells Wren House, and Mimi and Lautner move in with him in the Bryanston Square flat. He is in a fever to do something (sell the company, move here or there) but settles on inviting Dolly, Hal, Nettie, and Will on a Mediterranean cruise so successful that it is repeated for the next five years.

The last picture in the album is of another wedding, that of George and Ursie. The clue to what has settled Alfred forms the final lines of the novel:

Here is Alfred, tall, stiff, still a handsome man. Here is Nettie, very close to Alfred, leaving Will [her husband] almost unattached, unpaired. And in the front row, the three children: Laurie, Charlie [who belong to Lili and Benjie], and Nettie's child Vicky (Victoria). See that look on Vicky's face, that imperious stare, so unlike a child, so like Sofka. See Alfred's hand proudly clasping her little shoulder. See the resemblance. Wait for the dancing to begin. (187)

At the wedding celebrated in the opening photograph, Alfred has "danced" with his cousin Nettie, Dolly's half-sister. They have always liked each other. He has read and reread the postcards she sent him, and she had hoped that he would be waiting for her when she returned from her finishing school in Switzerland. They both remember their childhood, when they were close, as the best time they have had and long to recapture its essence. Neither Nettie nor Dolly has children, a fact "inexplicable, unless you believe in those old superstitions about the wrong partner producing no children" (170). Then apparently during the years of those Mediterranean cruises, a miracle happened: Nettie, whose "still red hair shone like a marigold in the fierce sun" (180) on board ship, gets pregnant. Clearly Vicky is Alfred's daughter. Clearly of all Sofka's progeny, Alfred has been the true child of his father, managing at the last to protect the family and play the renegade. "Leaning on the guardrail, surveying the next port of call, he [Alfred] appeared to reflect that compromise is not a bad solution, and that modified escape does not destroy the possibility of return" (180–81). It is a lesson that Ruth Weiss of *The Debut* and, especially, Kitty Maule of *Providence* never learned; Edith Hope, of *Hotel du Lac,* with her secret life, is rather more like Alfred.

The Daughters: The Excellent and the Unprincipled

Family and Friends has the most extensive portraits to date of the opposite of the excellent women who are usually Brookner heroines, and it allows us to see, close in, that they are less golden than they appear and no more successful, finally, than their opposites, who so admire them and would emulate them if they could. Mimi's younger sister, Betty, is the most unprincipled major character in the novel, and naturally her mother finds her far more interesting than the good daughter, Mimi. At the end of the novel, we realize that, structurally, Brookner has established Betty's failure from the opening, for, in that first family portrait, the "daughters are in white, with ribbons in their long hair, which I [the narrator] know to have been red" (7), and, near the end, in the last vignette of Betty, reduced to a quiet life in attendance on her husband, Max, who has suffered a heart attack and will never work very much again, Betty wanders down to the pool and stares into the water. "Isn't it a pretty colour?" she says forlornly to the man who has come to filter it. 'I had a hair ribbon just that shade when I was a little girl' " (164). Another of Sofka's children—and one who has escaped her mother's tyranny—remembers her childhood fondly. We are likely to remember the similar kind of effective circularity that frames *Look at Me* and *The Debut*.

Betty is the only one of Sofka's children born to rebel, and her mother does indeed trace the wild strain in her and her cousins Dolly and Nettie to "that recessive gene that ordains seductive eyes and a sharp expression," "leavens the ordinary good behaviour" of the family, and "points the way to will and to satisfaction" (115). Always favoring the performance of songs too old for her and born possessed of a "guttersnipe charm" (32), she, from practically her childhood, intends to run away and be a dancer at the Folies-Bergères. The cat images with which Brookner consistently treats her relate to slyness rather than kittenishness. Uninterested in literature and studies, she ironically looks like the author Colette, a likeness that is even more pronounced when she sneaks away to have her red hair cut in a style that makes her look older than her years. And she does play the role for which her looks cast her. When Betty turns eighteen, she and Mimi, then twenty, receive a thousand pounds each through their father's arrangements, and she is able to dress to suit herself: "With the ivory cigarette-holder between her teeth and her fingernails painted bright red, with her legs crossed high, her brooding eyes and her sharp teeth, Betty looks like a painting by Foujita, a native Parisian, a Bohemian, a fallen angel" (40). Even Sofka comes to refer to the absent Betty as her "Gypsy" and to excuse her accordingly. She plays to her looks too, first on the dance floor at Mr. Cariani's where she meets Frank, who teaches the tango, rumba, and cachucha, and determines to use him as part of her escape plot. He "looks like a wild creature whose nakedness is struggling to dominate his unaccustomed trappings" but is "quite a good fellow, quite decent" (35). Betty's looks mirror her nature:

Betty is a good dancer but she is a much better actress. She is acting the part of a passionate and scornful woman of Mediterranean habits and lineage, whereas she is in fact the milky-complexioned child of reclusive Europeans. As she strives to adapt her virgin body and her complicated and corrupt temperament to the Latin steps, her face takes on the precise and moody urgency of a Parisian artist's model. (36)

Betty's cousin Nettie is also something of a problem for her parents (though the Nettie of the latter part of the book seems so different that we wonder if perhaps Dolly would not have been the better choice), and she is sent to a finishing school in Switzerland to be tamed. Sofka makes the same arrangements for Betty, who has different plans. When she sees the look of interest and liking exchanged between Mimi and Frank, who is targeted as the instrument by means of which she will acquire what she wants, she immediately launches her plan: foiling her mother's attempts by tricking the lazy Frederick into leaving her on her own in Paris, where she promptly takes up residence rather than catching the train to school. It is Mimi who tracks her down, makes the arrangements for her to receive money through the family agent, and soothes matters at home, though she makes an abortive effort to regain Frank.

Betty is generally without scruples, and we begin to believe that the bad do live happily ever after. The instinct that brought her to Paris is apt, and by the time Mimi finds her in a café-bar, she has purchased a cheap fur jacket and become at one with the exotica of her surroundings. Brash to the point that she amuses almost every man she meets, she has demanded and gotten an audition at the Moulin Rouge. She uses her standard techniques, "sparkling" (applied by Sally "Beamish" to Patrick in *The Misalliance*) and "pouting" (66), to withhold Frank from Mimi. Although he is used to women behaving in this way toward him, Frank succumbs and falls in love with her. Always uncomfortable with the "slightly disagreeable undertones of this adventure" (65), he tries in vain to get her to marry him, but he is useful only as an escort and as a partner in *Bunny et Frank, danseurs de charme* (89) until she recognizes that he is the star of the act and turns her attention to the pursuit of a film career, another thirst as yet unfulfilled. A "healthy animal" with the "gift" of a "sense of well-being" (90), she values only acclaim and quickly recognizes that she can achieve almost as much by her habitual body language without having to perform the labor required in dancing. More sensual even than Frederick, she loves her days in Paris and is more Parisian than the Parisians.

Again with that never-flagging Brookner gift for irony, Betty, believing herself a femme fatale, though while some men are excited by her "slightly sharp odour" (which her brother Alfred detests), most are amused by her posturing, is outdone by love. She manages to meet a Hungarian film producer who, she thinks, will be her passport to America. And so he is, for he too is amused by her and sees that she will be a success on the screen as a bad girl. However, Betty is not prepared for his nephew, who, her soulmate in catliness, is "the cruel-eyed lover of her dreams" and "a splendid feral creature with a narrow glossy head and dark plum-coloured eyes" (94). A poseur herself, she exposes her inexperience by supposing Max to be derisive and to have a volcanic temperament. In fact, though as appealing to women as Frank Cariani, he is insecure and merely has hit upon gestures and ways (such as his bluster) consistently misinterpreted by women as more sinister than they are. Her appetite gains ascendancy over her wish to manipulate. She knows that she will never control a man like Max but does not, for once, care. Her concern, rather, since she does not exert the control, is how to move them to where she wants to be: enacting her precocious and long-lived sexual fantasies with this man. With Max's sexual conquest of her, the image she has affected becomes reality. When her appetite for Max abates, she will, she believes, move on to something else, for she is one of those "self-renewing persons" (87) who can discard whatever or whoever disappoints and go on to the next conquest.

In Max, however, Betty is mistaken. Their origins are similar. Like many other Europeans, including the Dorn family (before it was transplanted to England) and Lautner, Max's mother is beset by "wars and rumors of wars" and begs her brother, who has already fled, to save her son. Uncle and nephew bring with them from the Old Country images of life in the streets, which Max will ultimately use to great advantage in his television series about a fugitive from the police; he will indeed draw on the emptiness he has experienced "back home" to become a "creative cineaste" (158). They both also bring a love of upper-middle-class European manners and ways that are strangely like those of Sofka. If Betty never misses her family, though she occasionally thinks of her mother and particularly of the fact that, when Sofka dies, she will be the favorite of no one (161), Max, with Lautner, becomes increasingly fascinated by the Dorns precisely as family. Betty is impatient with his constant attentiveness to the Dorn portraits she receives once they are in America; they are "like a dream of home to him" (160), as the term *Mama* "means all the world to Lautner. It means coming home" (168).

Betty resents too the life reflected in those photographs. The Dorns left behind in England are rich, she feels, and are deliberately withholding her share of the family fortune. If they wanted her to come home to a wedding, they should send tickets. Her life with Max has not been all she imagined. Her first discomfort in her marriage was their removal from New York, where she had paraded up and down Madison, Park, and Fifth avenues in the fur coat Mr. Markus, Max's uncle, had bought her. Instinctively she knew that Hollywood would be different; for one change, she would not be able to wear her fur coat there. And although Max was among the first to see the possibilities in television, neither he nor his uncle has been so successful in movies as is their due. Accordingly the career she felt promised and intended for has not materialized. Her sultriness no longer in vogue, she has been offered nothing more than a cameo as a waitress and has fallen back—again the Brooknerian irony—on reading, though for the selfish reason of carving a niche for herself by finding material for Max. In fact, she merely bores him to death by detailing the plot of each novel she reads. Her sexual coarseness has only momentarily enslaved Max (whereas her brother Frederick continues to be held in sway by Evie). Though she is not aware of them, Max in fact, like her father, has occasional affairs. She also does not know that what attracted him to her was her self-obsession, her tendency to ignore even him until she needed him, and "that wild unstudied side of her nature that could turn, with equally keen appetite, from simple physical greed to the stern and unforgiving appraisal of her appearance before some evening party, when at her dressing-table, she would moisten her lips, narrow her eyes, take up her mirror and study her reflection from every angle" (152). After Max's heart attack, Betty spends her time castigating the selfishness of people, especially her family, forgetting that she left Paris without telling Frank. Although she does not remember Lautner, who came to the Dorns' weekly when she was a child, she is glad that Mimi did not get Frank. It has never occurred to her that there is anything wrong with sending home her secondhand clothes as gifts. All she knows is that she is simply "not having the good time she always promised herself" (151). Until the exile brought on by Max's health, life was buying clothes and changing them several times a day, being more contentious than the other Hollywood wives, and getting her way by fits of ill humor.

On one level, Frederick and Betty, the reprobates, have won. Both have generally good marriages in the sense that the partners match. Evie not only suits but plays to Frederick's needs. Max would not have

the Sofka and Mimi kind of wife who sees that her husband's shirts are
well laundered and are scented with "lavender and vetiver" (the leitmotif in this novel for the Sofka and Mimi Old World world). If both end
in permanent exile, Frederick is self-contented, though we may find
him too limited to perceive that he has been taken over by Evie. Betty
is exiled in Hollywood, a city of fugitives and exiles among whom talk
of the Old World is unacceptable and a city equally alien to what
becomes her favorite theme, her childhood. From the self-induced and
self-sought exotica of Paris, she finds herself "permanently exiled" in a
"hot and characterless garden" (151) in Beverly Hills. When Max dies,
she will never go home again: "Some old trouper's pride will keep her
sitting here, by the pool, to the very end" (184).

For all the thought she lends to her past and her childhood, Betty
never finds insight. She has used her sister only as a foil: "Where once
she had only to display herself against the dreamy passivity of her sister
Mimi" (to produce a "sense of effortless superiority"), she is now surrounded by women of her own type, all of them, according to Betty,
"lacking in humanity" (159). Self-exiled, she has no hope of regaining
her advantage over Mimi, though Mimi herself has finally evolved into
a Sofka type. The best Betty can do is dye her hair a vivid red in
memory of its former glory. The best she and Frederick can do is,
separately, to condemn Alfred the Man of Property and Mimi the
Matriarch, never once questioning what has happened to their own
"wild card" and "ludic impluse":

Who could have foretold the ultimate passivity of Frederick and of Betty,
subsiding into the permanence of what was originally a temporary arrangement, with a backward glance only to the mythic elements of their own lives?
How have these artists in self-referral managed to edit themselves into a
version so static, and yet so emblematic, that those at home, who have not
seen them for many years, have no difficulty at all in picturing them, Frederick in his linen jacket and his panama hat and his pale shoes, smiling and
strolling and savouring his pleasures, the boulevardier of his mother's imagination, and Betty, cross-grained and vivid in her flimsy clothes, eternally toying
with something coloured in a long glass, and glancing down critically at her
painted toenails? (185)

To a great extent, Betty (with Frederick) has ended up in the pattern of
the comforting vignette she used to watch from her Parisian flat of

women eating cakes in the softly lit interior of the patisserie opposite, an image Betty has seen as woman's true destiny, though thinking that her own life would be much more exciting and demanding (88). Betty has seen an image, and her life has been shaped to fit it.

In *Family and Friends*, both sisters, the good and the bad, have red hair, as if Brookner, slightly mocking, were treating us to "red hair is as red hair does." She again plays on a woman's letting down her hair (or, here, cutting it) as a moral commentary. Betty cuts hers early and against the family's wishes and ages herself accordingly. On the afternoon before she awaits Frank Cariani in her hotel room, Mimi tries to get her hair cut. The hairdresser admires and refuses to touch it. Instead he brushes it "amorously," and she sees herself as Rossetti's "Beata Beatrix." She "submits" to having it washed, dried, and "her chignon put up again" (70); symbolically, her act of giving herself to her lover, of attracting her lover to her, has already failed. Mimi is on her way to being the old maid who will marry, at age thirty-five, a man as old as her father.

In Paris, Mimi sheds her fears and nervousness for the only time in her life. She knows that Betty is lost to the family forever and is ready to center her whole life on a struggle with her sister to get Frank back. She literally does just that: centers her entire life on the effort. Brookner has her return to her childhood as a way of girding her loins for the encounter. Prior to going to Betty's hotel, she walks in the Tuileries gardens as she used to with her nurse when she accompanied her parents to Paris and, "like a child," "stoops and picks up a chestnut, green, prickly, and hard, too young to split and reveal its glossy fruit" (61; a favorite Brookner image). She knows too that she has "somehow come into her own" (62). We begin to think that here is a Brookner woman who will stand up for herself and rebel against the role thrust upon her. Here is a Brookner woman who will give a rightful comeuppance to her oppressor (Betty). She not only sees that she looks like the Lady of Shalott by comparison with her sister but that "she should do something about it" (64). She continues her new-found valor by winning from Frank the acknowledgment that he has always liked her more than Betty and then tells him she will wait at her hotel. Suddenly she is the standard Brookner woman again, pinning volumes of life on a gesture of or a word from or the performance of a male type. In this instance, Mimi has imbibed a dream of the masculine from her father (and fed it with the mythic image of the lover):

She was always secretly conscious of being his favourite and from the memory
of his hand stroking her long red hair or producing chocolates for her from a
silver box [an object paralleling the cigarette box in *Look at Me*] she has learnt
to yearn for that aura of masculinity which intrigues a woman, tempts her, and
makes her long to satisfy her curiosity. With Mimi, this is all below the
surface, far below. She only knows that at home with Sofka and Frederick and
Alfred and recently Betty she has been questing unconsciously for that man,
that alien, that stranger, that appointed one, who will deliver her, the sleep-
walker, from her sleep. Thus, in the bosom of her family, Mimi, the good
daughter, has been the one most ready, most willing, to defect. (69)

In a dreamlike but highly conscious state, she dresses and waits in her
hotel room for Frank to come, fully assured that she has not already
missed him and certain in her knowledge of the steps in the encounter.
When it grows late, she "is suddenly overtaken by the much stronger
impression that he will now steal into her room like a lover, like a thief
in the night" (71). She takes down her hair and puts on her plain white
gown to wait. When the episode is over, she sinks into a malaise from
which she never fully recovers, and she never returns to Paris. Her life
is stunted by this failed imagined romantic interlude. Until she is
persuaded by Sofka to marry old Lautner, she passes her time in doing
good works at the hospital. Languorous and self-effacing, she, like
Blanche Vernon of the upcoming *The Misalliance,* suffers from headaches. She is never hungry, and her magnificent red hair seems merely
to drag her down (shades of Ruth Weiss in *The Debut*). She is even
tyrannized over by Alfred's housekeeper, Muriel, whom Mimi assists as
if she herself were a minor domestic in the household. She "feels invisi-
ble" and lives a "nun-like existence" (126). Her mother wants her to
sing Betty's stock piece, "Les Filles de Cadiz"; the result is another
"failed attempt" (125).

Fate (and Brookner) will not allow Mimi to escape by being a nonen-
tity and by willing herself to live at the level of surface value and think
well of everyone but herself. To her horror, she sees Betty's "annexa-
tion" of Frank Carini being reenacted by Dolly with Alfred. The scene
forces from her an admission, once again, that "the world is a jungle,
filled with humans no less rapacious than the animals" (116). The
imagery is very close to that of Margaret Drabble's young heroine in *A
Summer Bird-Cage;* the tone is infinitely darker and more frightening.
Mimi pays with another migraine headache.

Fate will not stop having its way with Mimi. Once reconciled to marriage for the sake of marriage (a choice Edith Hope has refused in *Hotel du Lac*), she becomes as forceful as Sofka. Pregnant at forty, she enjoys the best health of her life. Then an evilly grinning fate turns on her; her mother dies, and she loses the baby with the shock. A long illness is followed by a lapse into "that depression, that irradiation of the spirit, that had afflicted her so long ago on her return from Paris" (181). She revives only when Alfred moves Lautner and her back to Bryanston Square with him. If her cup ever runs over, it will run over "with decency rather than with anything more *vital*" (181; my italics). Only readers of Anita Brookner would hear the irony in that statement. Mimi's life settles into a routine of "good management" replete with "lavender and vetiver" and "the journals . . . all uncreased on the table in the study": "perhaps her true *apotheosis* [another clue in Brookner to failed expectations], this return to the still intact dreams of her girlhood" (182). Another of Sofka's children relives her childhood. How dare Brookner suggest that Sofka was not a good mother! It is, finally, this best of the four children whose life has most in consonance with the quotation from Goethe's *The Sorrows of Young Werther* that forms the epigraph:[8]

There is much to be said for the advantage of rules and regulations, much the same thing as can be said in praise of middle-class society—he who sticks to them will never produce anything that is bad or in poor taste, just as he who lets himself be moulded by law, order and prosperity will never become an intolerable neighbour or a striking scoundrel. On the other hand . . . rules and regulations ruin our true appreciation of nature and our powers to express it.

Mimi knows that her well-regulated life is better not examined. Since she lost her baby, the music that used to be her solace upsets her and causes headaches. She jettisons the piano and tries to avoid thinking about the "if only's" of her life.

The Novel as Novel

Some critics have praised Brookner's fifth novel as her best,[9] but no one seems to have taken much notice of the move she has made here to male characters. In contrast, when Margaret Drabble brought out *The Needle's Eye,* critics immediately recognized the sudden shift to a sharing of the central focus by Rose and Simon, although she had already been inside the heads of minor male figures. *Family and Friends* is another novel of contemporary manners,[10] but it is different in the way that it enlists a narrative device, the viewing of a series of photographs, to provide a family chronicle that leads to a variation on Brookner's accustomed novel of character—here, indeed, a novel of five major characters: Sofka and her four children. The device is a natural enough one for Brookner the art critic and reminds us of the pictorial material with which Frances Hinton works in *Look at Me. Family and Friends* also draws on the world of art for analogues.[11]

Family and Friends is among the oddest of Anita Brookner's generally odd novels, though it is also probably the best example in the canon of her almost uncanny ability to exact interest and variety from character types.[12] Its oddest feature is the point of view, particularly the erratic appearances of a first-person narrator who sounds as though he or she is a member of the Dorn family, never materializes or comes to much at all,[13] but is omnipresent nonetheless. Describing Sofka in the opening photograph as looking as though she thinks little of her brood beyond giving birth to them, for example, the narrator declares, "This I know to be the case" (8). We are finally left with the impression that Brookner is drawing on her own past life and apparently odd relationship with her exotic family. She is, in fact, as unforthcoming about the origins of the characters in *Family and Friends* as about her own biography, an approach that intrigues her readers and critics, though we probably feel that she is not trying to entice so much as to prevent revelation. We sense an almost painful kind of reticence about the author and her novels. On the basis of the scantiest of evidence, we project that the Dorns and their friends have left Eastern and Central Europe, are "(very faintly) Jewish,"[14] and are living in London between the world wars (in the period from about the 1920s to the late 1940s) while the children grow into their forties. Some have criticized in particular the inattentiveness to milieu: "It is hard to take seriously a novel, even a resolutely domestic novel, in which the Second World War occurs, in effect, offstage. (Please do not bring up Jane Austen; Napoleon was not bombing Bath.)"[15] Finally, given the feeling of withholding evidence that laces all of the novels, we cannot excuse the ignoring of setting as a structural device to produce a stylized world of "lavender and vetiver" and of the "silver bonbonnière filled with almonds and muscatels" (127), a hothouse world of Sofka's construction and self-focus, though at least one critic has commented on the fact that "there is a closeness of atmosphere, almost claustrophobic, in *Family*

and Friends, as if we were alternating between a discreetly perfumed
lady's boudoir and the smoking room of a superior gentlemen's club."[16]
On the other hand, one of the quite effective techniques by which
Brookner measures the movement of the world of the children away
from that of Sofka is her increasing attachment, as she ages and is
dying, to Lautner, who maintains the old ways of a world now largely
gone:

Lautner notices little things that the nurse misses. The fine linen handkerchief
has been creased; he will put a fresh one into the hand that lies inert on the lace
counterpane. He will sprinkle a little mimosa scent on the lamp, to make the
room smell of spring. He will touch Sofka's lips with glycerine and rosewater,
so that they do not become too dry. And although she no longer responds, he
will tell her in pleasant detail of the weather outside, describe for her the
position of Dorn and Co. on the stock-market, sometimes read her an item
from the newspaper: the weather in Nice, in Los Angeles. She likes to see him
sitting there, with his newspaper. She likes this reminder of the masculine
world, so authoritative, so reassuring, so unlike the tempestuous and secret
comings and goings of Alfred [who thus, like her other son, has been "femi-
nized"]. (167)

The Old World European strain in Brookner is largely absent in Barbara Pym and Margaret Drabble and, especially in its full flowering in
Family and Friends, has caused a feeling of strangeness: "It is, I have to
confess, an England I can barely recognize."[17]
    The texture, on the other hand, is virtually flawless. Un-English the
world of the novel may be, but what is depicted is depicted with
gemlike clarity. The words themselves can be not only apt but strik-
ingly original; for example, in the solitude of the early morning in the
Tuileries gardens, Mimi "is able to notice the *bones* of a landscape that
was previously hidden to her by a press of people" (61; my italics); "if
spirit is not too *discarnate* a word" (117–18; my italics). Even a recurrent interest in an image is appealing here: "Mimi drifts noiselessly
under the chestnut trees, now heavy with the last of their green leaves;
already the sap has left them and the brown and gold colours have
begun their invasion. Like a child, Mimi stoops and picks up a chestnut, green, prickly, and hard, too young to split and reveal its glossy
fruit" (61). It is an excellent small disquisition on what Brookner
herself is doing in *Family and Friends.* Especially in this novel, Brookner
is able to carom off her established device; the narrator's viewing of an
occasional picture allows a zooming in on one character and a concomi-

tant buildup by repetition, as when we are brought into the picture and the story with this focus on Lautner: "See how patriarchally he places encompassing arms on the back of the sofa on which Mimi is seated! See how he stands when she enters the room and opens the door when she leaves it!" (182).

Here too is the accustomed use of foils not only as structural devices of the author but as conscious ploys by the characters. One of the reasons that Dolly has chosen Hal as her husband, for example, is that his "plainness" "sets off her extraordinary colouring" (112). Again, they may not know the word but instinctively see the effect of its use, as when "gradually Frank accepts that his perfect and unemphatic [dance] movements are merely a *foil* for Betty's more complex attitudes" (36; my italics). Vignette is also operative when Betty takes the scene in the pastry shop as a symbol of what a woman's life should be. If *Family and Friends* is another novel in which the quest to be viable is uppermost, Brookner has nonetheless proved that this is a human's rather than a woman's need only.

Chapter Seven
The Misalliance: "The Fibrous Content of Real Life"

The Human Continuum

Ironically, given the search for fulfillment through a man that is a constant with Brookner heroines, the title of the sixth novel, *The Misalliance* (1986), refers principally to a relationship that Blanche Vernon has tried to effect with an approximately three-year-old child, Elinor or Nelly, in the period following her separation, some two years earlier, and ultimate divorce, from Bertie.[1] After twenty years of marriage, he moved in with Amanda or "Mousie," "a young woman [twenty years his junior] with a degree in computer sciences" "in whom [Blanche] can discern not the slightest spark of imagination" but who is "all he ever wanted" and who has given him "a new lease on life" (5, 16)—male clichés but devastating in effect nonetheless. Before the novel is over, we are likely to be thinking that the real misalliance was with Bertie; when it is over, we are likely to be thinking that the next misalliance is with Bertie—who, in an exceedingly well-done surprise ending, returns to Blanche.

We are given not so much insights into the marriage as into the character of Blanche, which changed in accordance with her perceptions of what Bertie wanted her to be. Again the heroine is a woman of independent means and good works. A great difference from the usual Brookner protagonist is that she learns to need other people (among them, Mrs. Duff, her virtuous neighbor; Miss Sylvia Elphinstone, the domestic, an "excellent woman" in the Barbara Pym mode), as much to help them as herself. Actually Blanche has made herself, in some ways, into a kind of learned fool, at least in the eyes of her acquaintances. Halted by marriage in her march to dondom, she has continued to accumulate quaint and wonderful lore (Plato, the labors of Hercules, the sun as God) that she puts into play, to the puzzlement of others and herself. Alone, she spends much of her time visiting places of edification, for example, the National Gallery, whose nymphs seem to come to life in the majority of women around her, particularly Mousie and Sally Beamish, stepmother to Elinor.

The Misalliance is a case study of Blanche Vernon, but, as usual, Brookner establishes the full female continuum, without a character at the center. In this novel, she also places all of us on the human continuum that she has been working toward throughout her fiction. The title thus has ironic reference too to our tendency to misplace ourselves, to misalign. On the one end are the good women: Blanche, Mrs. Duff, and Miss Elphinstone; on the other are the predators: Mousie and Sally Beamish but also, in the stunning variation of this novel on the Brookner pattern, the world of pagan art, particularly the kouroi of the British Museum, and in the wake of these two groups, all of the rest of us if we have not already perceived our places:

She saw suddenly and precisely something that had previously only appeared to her in a vague and nebulous light: a great chasm dividing the whole of womanhood. On the one side, Barbara [Bertie's sister] with her bridge evenings and her gouty husband, Mrs Duff with her girlish respectability, and her own awkward self, and on the other Mousie and her kind and Sally Beamish, movers and shakers, careless and lawless, dressed in temporary and impractical garments, and in their train men who would subvert their families, abandon their wives and children, for their unsettling companionship. On the one side the evangelical situation—and Miss Elphinstone too came into it at this point—and on the other the pagan world. For "good" women, Blanche thought, men would present their "better" selves, saving their primitive and half-conscious energies for the others. And she herself, she further thought, had made the mistake of trying to fashion herself for the better half, assuming the uncomplaining and compliant posture of the Biblical wife [the model for Mrs. Duff also and for Sofka in *Family and Friends* and Dorrie in *A Friend from England*] when all the time the answer was to be found in the scornful and anarchic posture of the ideal mistress. (63–64)

Another fillip is added with the presentation of the men in the book as foils for each other, as well as for the types on the continuum. Patrick Fox, who belongs on the good women end of the spectrum, has rivaled Bertie for Blanche and in the course of the novel tries to move to the bad women category represented by Sally Beamish but lacks the constitution to make the change. Bertie, who moves from Blanche to Mousie, cannot sustain the effort. Clever, too, is Brookner's letting her heroine not only be aware of continua and foils but verbalize them. Indeed, they throw into relief miniature misalliances and thus provide more interpretations of the book's title. Blanche eschews such extremes of the continuum as vice and virtue and sees the struggle, in terms originating with Brookner, as "between effectiveness and futility or between vitality and inertia"—"And somewhere in the middle of these conflicting principles, she saw the man, uncommitted, easily beguiled, *volage*" (119).

What is missing from the parade of characters in Blanche's world (and the world of Brookner's novels) is a male who is a match for Sally, Mousie, and the nymphs. Both Frederick, initially, and Alfred, finally, fail to be so in *Family and Friends*, and they are far more successful at the type than Nick in *Look at Me*. The trouble is that they are attracted to the Sallys and Mousies or to the mythology they seem to represent but finally belong to the more circumscribed world. In *The Misalliance*, one of the greatest and most ironic referents of the title is the mixing of these dichotomous mythologies. If Blanche learns about Mousie from learning about Sally, another misalliance, she also learns about Bertie from learning about Sally's husband, Paul, whom she comes to contrast with Sally: "whereas Paul, now that she came to think of it, had exactly the unthinking placatory attitude that doomed him in his quest for strength. Paul, to a certain extent, was Adam. His trouble was that he had got mixed up in the wrong mythology. Sally . . . would go on to other partners: Paul would be stuck with Mrs Demuth, with Mr Demuth always at hand to castigate him. It was a situation which could not be resolved" (158). Similarly, Patrick, the most reliable male in the book and the one most like Blanche, succumbs to the forbidden fruit of Sally, who would use him when Blanche seems to be failing her: "Patrick's smile had faded; his flirtatious proposals were quite in abeyance. Suddenly Blanche was aware that he was a middle-aged man, putting on weight, no longer as eligible in appearance as he once had been, and, she saw, unequal to this situation" (106–7).

What does all this teach her about Bertie? Not very much because she still tends to absorb too much of the blame. We begin to applaud when she takes him to at least small task for looking terrible, needing a haircut, and wearing a shirt that "would look loud on a juvenile" (110). Her trouble is that, as with the case of the art she constantly studies, she misreads the cues or, rather, fashions them after her own slant. She appears to have remade herself into what she supposed Bertie wanted her to be without ever asking him or doing any reality checks. She knows that he is actually as conventional as she is and hates fuss as much as she does. When he tells her about the crowded living conditions of his and Mousie's trip to Corfu, she marvels, remembering him "as a man of the utmost fastidiousness, filling the bathroom with smells of verbena and sandalwood" (169), but she does not outwardly respond. She is so caught up in her own desire to keep a stiff upper lip that she credits his visits to his feeling sorry for her and wanting to prevent her committing suicide. She does not recognize that he not only misses her regular and very good meals and well-kept house but misses her, is jealous of Patrick, and is dropping hints. She has, after all, surprised them both by admitting that she still loves him, and we suspect that she has never before said such a thing to him out of fear of offending. When she raises the idea that he and Mousie will marry and that she will go away and give them the flat, he encourages her not to change and says that her standards were always too high. She thinks that a rebuke; we are more likely to read it as his apology for not measuring up. In fact, he catches at her arm and would probably have started the reconciliation then and there, but she turns away, still too decorous and too desirous of appearing self-sufficient. He leaves on the note that he was never "half-hearted" (176).

If we except *Family and Friends,* which stands out as the most unusual novel of the Brookner canon, the heroine of *The Misalliance* is different from her sisters in the other novels only in having been married. As they consider their ineffectualness to be their own fault, she feels shame for her divorce and puts on a good front by bearing her load "nobly" while being "humbled, baffled, and innocent" (5) and by dressing impeccably: "And when the worst did happen she merely threw it off with as much amused laughter as she could muster and determined to improve herself so that nothing could afflict her again, thinking, again mistakenly, that some unworthiness in herself had brought this about, and that if she improved she would be rewarded" (88). Besides, she "calculate[s] that she [can] spend up to an unwanted hour every morning by simply putting herself to rights, and producing a pleasing effect to lavish on the empty day" (7). Her principal useful occupation is "keeping feelings at bay," as we learn in the opening sentence of the novel. Where her sisters work and have most difficulty passing their nights, she, like Mimi in *Family and Friends,* has only her volunteer work at the hospital, which "fed her seriousness" (6). She makes it a "matter of honour to be busy and amused until darkness f[alls] and release[s] her from her obligations"; leaving home is the event of her day (5). She summons up a "particularly quizzical tolerance in order to keep panic at bay" (6), and it serves rather to make her even more remote and unapproachable. Given to such vocabulary as *behooves,* she acts on what "it behooves one to do in the circumstances."

The same question obtains here: are women, even a few, much less the majority, really like those in Brookner's novels? While the craftsmanship of the author and the authenticity of the construct keep us from questioning the basic premise in them that, yes, most women are like Blanche Vernon and Kitty Maule in being so unsure of themselves and so certain that they are at fault no matter what the case or the problem, once out of the book or removed from it momentarily, we are likely to be incredulous. How could any contemporary woman, particularly one like Blanche, with individual means, some knowledge of the brighter social world, and a partially written thesis on Mme de Staël[2] started apparently before her marriage, remake herself in the image she thinks her husband demands? While good marriages (and good relationships generally) assuredly require some accommodation on the part of both parties, all give and all take are surely long since outmoded. Yet here is Blanche, so happy to be married that she has consciously curbed her exuberance and "cultivated tastes which she felt instinctively to be thin, sharp, brittle, like the very dry sherry which Bertie assumed that she liked as well as he did" (6). Even after the marriage is ostensibly over, she still looks "on him, as she had always looked on him, as a kind of gigantic treat, a prize won in a lottery, something fortunate and undeserved, and, because undeserved, all the more pleasurable" (36). With his loss, she experiences, in slightly different terms, the sense of being almost nonexistent that plagues other Brookner women: "Blanche thought of herself as no age at all, as dematerialized, made hollow by his disappearance" (36). Only in him has she seen "intimations of her own validity, as if without him that validity disappeared" (a play on Wordsworth's "intimations of immortality" perhaps), though she knows that this is not the way "for a self-respecting modern woman to feel" (173). Her whole post-Bertie life nonetheless is a sham; she "turned to flirtations with other lives, good works, and uplifting pastimes" but only to impersonate "worthiness" and to try to "learn the art of self-sufficiency." From Blanche's point of view, all else since Bertie is "misalliance" (173).

Though to a far lesser extent in this novel than is Brookner's custom, Blanche has shaped her role as married woman after the patterns cut in literature and the lore that Brookner suggests to be passed from generation to generation, some great imprinting by the "female unconscious." Ironically Patrick has tended to read the same fiction as she; thus, if she had married him, they would still be married (94). On the other hand, she is sure that they differ in their understanding of marriage, which he, no doubt, would see in the classical manner as a "reflection of the divine harmony," while "to her, marriage was a form of higher education, the kind that other women gained at universities. And she supposed that on her better days she would have got quite a good degree. Patrick, however, would expect her to get a First every day of the year" (95). Her former sister-in-law, Barbara, who likes her and maintains ties with her, recognizes that Blanche is eccentric, "always dressed to the nines, making elliptical remarks," and "carrying on about characters in fiction, or characters whom she said should be in fiction" (16, 17). The case is, rather, that Blanche, with very limited experience upon which to draw in her efforts to please Bertie and his friends by "edit[ing] herself into a more worldly version," has turned to "works of fiction" that have not been sufficient:

She could see that Bertie was an avid social animal but not how far his animality would take him. It came as a complete surprise to her to learn that Bertie was fascinated by Mousie, because Mousie simply did not figure in her list of characters. Men who fell in love with their secretaries, even if they had the decency or the prudence to move those secretaries to another position, were, to her, characters from another kind of fiction, the kind she did not read. She supposed this secondary kind of fiction to be as powerful and as pervasive as folklore because everyone apart from herself seemed to know about it. (93–94)

Having found literature, at least real literature, a failure, she has looked to art and begun to find patterns for the contemporary world. She has heretofore imagined that the pagan dispensation had merely been superseded by the Christian. Not so; the dichotomies of the pagan and the modern world are the same: "the discrepancy between duty and pleasure. On the one side the obedient, and on the other the free" (94).

Blanche also not only identifies the pagan world, Sally, and Mousie as children but places the child Elinor on the good women and futility end of the spectrum. In another variation also related to the child theme that runs through the novel, she perceives that the difference between Mousie and herself is being loved versus not being loved, the kind of privilege that attaches to the pretty throughout their lives (another constant note in Brookner's novels):

Metaphorically, Mousie had been holding out her arms, in the certainty of meeting a welcoming embrace, since she was a little girl. Even her nickname, Mousie, bestowed on her at that same early age, betokened spoiling, cherishing, a father's if not a mother's, indulgence [yet another allusion in Brookner to the sexual content in the relations between fathers and daughters]. By holding out her baby arms Mousie had emitted the correct signals: People knew what their response should be. And because she was so delightfully forthcoming, because she was so easy to understand, because she was so artlessly pleased with the response she invariably elicited, she was allowed to be equally artless when the response was perhaps a little lacking in fervour. Tears of rage would start up in her eyes, accusations would pour from her hotly, presents would be spurned. In this way she cemented attachment through guilt, and any discomfort that this might cause would be swept away by one of Mousie's lightning changes of mood, her gaiety, her demands for affection, of which she could apparently never have enough. Mousie needed to function from a position of emotional dominance; as this was an art which she had learnt in her cradle, and as it had worked so well at that time, she had seen no need to modify it throughout her adult life. (26–27)

Mousie is thus made in the image of every bad woman in the Brookner canon, but the great coup here is that the analysis is so beautifully tailored to Blanche, the repository of eccentric lore. Always a reader, she turns back to Plato and quaintly (but delightfully) adapts him to the case at hand:

If, as Plato says, all knowledge is recollection, she had always known that she would fail in this particular contest, for her own plainness as a child had caused her to look longingly at the delighted smiles bestowed on other, prettier little girls, and she had wished in vain to have a tantrum of her very own. But the tantrums of plain little girls do not have the desired effect, and by the time those plain little girls have grown up and become elegant women the art has been lost for ever because it has never been possessed. (31)

Her reading of Plato's *Philebus* in fact also fits the continuum structure through which Blanche is trying to work in the course of the novel. She reads "that the life of pleasure must be mixed with reason and the life of reason must be mixed with pleasure but that a third quality, to which both reason and pleasure look forward, must be the final ingredient of the good life" (162). Recognizing that she would gratefully settle for the "life of pleasure," she puts aside the dialogue without bothering to pursue what the third virtue is or to take the message that either-or categorizing does not make for the good life.

If Blanche finally condemns the world for such dichotomizing into tortoises and hares (the classification applied in *Hotel du Lac*), she is initially as taken in by the lures of the hares as anyone else. While there is "nothing of the predator" in her (45), she has chosen Bertie over Patrick precisely because he is a worse man (91); we learn that even Miss Elphinstone, "like many blameless women," loves a "disreputable man" and thus admires Bertie (23). In the courtship, Bertie ignored Blanche and placed her in a position of servility, while Patrick exhausted her with "his enormous respect for women and his irreproachable concern for her" (93). We are left to wonder how, if she recognizes this pull in herself, she can still question it in Bertie. Blanche never fully unravels the mystery of herself or the world. At most, we can applaud her questing for answers and for the sources where she hopes, if anywhere, to find them. Like most other Brookner characters, she is the victim of the ironist. If she did not expect art to console her, she did expect it to take her out of herself and finds rather that it keeps "return[ing] her to herself with no comment" (8), a fair rendering of what Brookner learned in writing her first novel: "It was an exercise in self-analysis . . . but what is interesting about self-analysis is that it leads nowhere—it is an art form in itself."[3] Haunting the museums, Blanche has fragments of her past thrown back at her and actually feels faint before the kouroi and their contrast with her on a "disappointing holiday in Greece" (9). They and the Goddess with the Pomegranate in Berlin embody and withhold all mystery. If she could understand them, she would know the secret of living in the world; she could be Ariadne willing Bacchus to leap from his chariot at her feet (16). As it is, she believes she knows that love was ordained by the old gods of antiquity for those they favored; all others live in a postlapsarian world where, daily, "one's partner, one's referent, one's *vis-à-vis,* the mirror of one's life" turns into "an acquaintance of uncertain intimacy, whose conversation, once so longed for, was, more often than not, alien, uneasy, resentful, and boring" (20). The closest she gets to the pagan world is "hearing the owl, Athena's attendant, hooting in the far distance" (21) to send her to bed by herself. She at best but parodies the rites of the pagan temple as she undergoes her "evening ritual of dispensation" and the "lustrations" (a second bath with essence of flowers) that will let her escape the day. She has "the anxious look, the lugubrious bleached look, on an inhabitant of mediaeval Flanders" and watches the pale shine of her "ribbed Gothic feet" as she rubs "embalming fluids" into her skin (21).

In *The Misalliance,* Brookner draws most heavily on the art world that has been her vocation, allowing Blanche Vernon to look to it for an interpretation of all life. What Blanche finds is that the saints seem to have suffered merely to be perfected in painting with only a symbol ("a tower or a key or a wheel") "as a dainty allusion to their sufferings" (53–54). The secret of success lies rather with the pagans whose "different code" (54) Blanche cannot decipher, but at least she knows that it exists and that it mocks the futility of the rest of us. When Blanche, under the attack of a migraine[4] (chapter 10) with the effort of trying to sort out the affairs of the Beamishes, moves into a higher, almost trancelike, state of consciousness, she achieves an epiphany of her own that at first leads her to the same conclusion as other Brookner heroines: "that the good live unhappily ever after" (*Family and Friends,* 183). Seeking comfort, she merely receives the same message written in the world of art and of all human mythologies:

When what she craved was an image of comfort, of succour, of forgiveness, and even—why not?—the face of a compassionate mother, or of any of those obscure saints who seek no martyrdom but are content with their humble destinies, she saw only the nymphs and deities who, apparently, in the world of art, inhabit the same heaven, sailing on clouds that seem to be moving faster when they are not freighted down with human hopes and prayers. In that sky, which is always blue, they sail, impervious to mortal needs, above the world of just deserts, leaving on earth the pilgrims seeking their glimpse of salvation. Forever in motion, as if buoyed on the thermals rising from the aspirations of the unenlightened, inscrutable, weightless. And the gods, striding with all their ideal muscularity into new liaisons, or smiting, wrestling, rising, setting, identifying with the cosmos of which they are embodiments, and bearing in their faces the ardour of the beginning of the world. (147)

In contrast stand Adam and Eve and all their progeny, including Blanche Vernon, the shame bearers, held to rules and "strangely unconscious of the wonders of creation" (148), and the self-conscious, the eternal tortoises whose "rules and regulations ruin our true appreciation of nature and our powers to express it," as Goethe puts it in the quotation from *The Sorrows of Young Werther* forming the epigraph of *Family and Friends.* Finally Blanche sees that we have no choice because the legacy of the pagan world withheld from us tortoises is eternal youth and "that time misspent in youth is sometimes all the freedom one ever has" (149). Sally will eventually lose her power to charm and extract. Already Blanche merely laughs at her when she snatches at the possibility of moving into Blanche's flat while she is away.

This recognition is a long time coming, however. The first flights to art result from Blanche's desire to find that the moments producing the happiest images of her past life still exist—and permanently—on canvas. What she thinks she has recognized is that "the knowing and impervious smiles of those nymphs" in the National Gallery have "more of an equivalence in ordinary life, as it is lived by certain women, then [*sic*] she had ever suspected" (88). Sally Beamish is such a nymph, more of a child than Elinor, but with an "archaic smile" (61) and a dirty flat, accustomed to having others, particularly men, come to her rescue. Sally and Mousie are the same type:

> For Sally, like Mousie, like those cynical smiling nymphs in the National Gallery, had known, with an ancient knowledge, that the world respects a predator, that the world will be amused by, interested in, indulgent towards the charming libertine. . . . Blanche knew herself to be part of the fallen creation, doomed to serve, to be faithful, to be honourable, and to be excluded. She saw that fallen creation, mournful in its righteousness, uncomforted in its desolation, and living in expectation, as she had waited long hours in her drawing-room for the hope that would not return. (79).

Another of the ironies lacing the book is the fact that the ultracontemporary Sally and Mousie live in the past in two ways, the first of which is their communion with the old pagan world of pleasure and irresponsibility. The second is Sally's animation only when in conditions of pleasure; she is completely passive and listless unless she has an audience for whom she can describe her suspension in a kind of "mythic time" when she and her companions "had all moved weightlessly from party to party, resort to resort," plying a "diet of hedonism, from which the fibrous content of real life had been removed" (77). In contrast, Blanche, the "old-fashioned" woman of old-fashioned values, learns to live in the present and to look for new images to cherish rather than doting on golden moments of her past: "Unlike Blanche, who thought in terms of the present ('Do it now!'), Sally lived entirely in the past, a past which she wished to see reproduced, in identical form, in the future" (100). Ironically Sally (with Elinor) becomes an inhabitant of the palace of the Sleeping Beauty (125), waiting to come back alive with her old life restored. Is her case any better than that of the majority of women—Cinderellas waiting for the prince? Ultimately Blanche does not want to be Sally Beamish or Mousie.

Blanche knows her strangeness and wants to conform to the proper type, though we wish that she could relish her individuality. Even her wine drinking is her own. She is a virtual connoisseur (e.g., Vouvray [15], Sancerre [33], Muscadet [72], Pirnot [82], Meursault [109], Sauternes [126], Piesporter [164], Frascati [190]). She is not just drinking because she feels sorry for herself; in fact, "Blanche, after two or three glasses, merely became calmer and displayed the rudiments of a sententious smile" (33). She believes that wine is "wasted on a meal," and Bertie says that she is the only person he knows "who thinks that cake is an accompaniment to wine" (110). She also finds champagne an inferior product (135). The fact that Blanche goes her own way with wine suggests, at least early in the novel, that she may retain her individuality and come to appreciate it, may learn to make a new point of reference for the human continuum. Blanche Vernon is *a* type and *no* type rather as Anita Brookner is *a* feminist and *no* feminist.

Children and Mothers

For a writer who is unmarried and has no children and whose heroines have no children, Anita Brookner pays unusual attention to children beyond the anticipated need of her protagonists to find their identities by breaking away from their parents. *The Misalliance* is especially filled with references to children. All of the good women in the novel are childless. Blanche and Mrs. Duff feel that their lives are blighted, in that respect, and Blanche comes upon her neighbor, with tears in her eyes, admiring a baby outside the post office. Miss Elphinstone, the old maid, is naturally childless; Blanche and Mrs. Duff, unnaturally so. The world is once more "cruel," this time "in apportioning children to the wrong mothers" (102).

The one child in the book, Elinor, is not the daughter of the woman, Sally, who passes as her mother, for her real mother died when she was born, and Blanche thinks the surrogate mother more of a child than Elinor: "Thus the whole principle of generation would be undersold, for Sally would never yield her place. Her place was to be young and to be the centre of attention. Mothers like this, as Blanche knew only too well, induce bewilderment, loneliness" (102). Blanche has to admit that Sally, though she has "the misleading facility of a woman who could do anything, but who lacked the wistfulness that betrays the woman who loves children" (117), can "educate [Elinor] to a sort of *viability*"[5] (102; my italics), that great raison d'être that the Brookner heroines long for and lack: "At the age of seven Elinor would be expected to be self-reliant; at the age of ten she would be given her sexual education; at the age of fifteen or sixteen she would be expected to have left home for good" (102). Meanwhile, Blanche, the would-be surrogate mother, will move out of the way and serve Elinor by setting up a trust fund for her to have at age seventeen, in effect proving the ironic viability of the type she will grow into under Sally's tutelage. As Blanche has supported Sally, she will support Elinor.

While the one crime for which Blanche does hold Bertie accountable is not giving her a child, her immediate response to Elinor is not as a surrogate daughter but as one whom Blanche might save from the clash of the two cultures she immediately sees embodied in the child and Sally. Elinor is so grave as to look like a foundling, another image from the stock of lore Blanche carts about, and contrasts sharply not only with the "pagan energy" (37) normal to children but with the "ichor of exreme and abundant youth and fertility" pulsing in the sheen of the skin of red-haired Sally (38), whose expression is the same as that of the nymphs in the National Gallery: "She had the smile of a true pagan. She would operate according to the laws of the old gods rather than huddle in the mournful companionship of the fallen world" (40). Blanche also believes that Elinor instinctively knows this unfairness of the world and admires her for rebelling against it by refusing to speak. Yet the child remains very fond of Sally and never very interested in Blanche, and, when she does finally speak, Sally remembers only that her words were related to her grandmother. Blanche has misconstructed the contours of Elinor's world along the misconstructions of her own; her alignments are wrong again. Wanting fellow-feeling with someone, she casts her own experience on Elinor, believing that the child is "earthbound" because Sally is so otherworldly and that the "blitheness" of Sally increases the "seriousness" of her stepdaughter (117). Moreover, knowing the paganness of Sally and thus her rightful expectation that, a Danae, she will have money pour from the heavens (129), Blanche nonetheless resents being used and having to pay for access to the child.

Blanche also misses the irony in Sally's last name, Beamish, for her own mantra—and the leitmotif of this novel—is "the sun is God" (7, 20, 96, 164). It helps her to move through the grayness of the London depicted in the book, and near the end she thinks of escaping to it in the south and being renewed. It is also dominant in her secret fantasies, "which she would have died rather than reveal," and her "vision of an alternate life":

If only I could live in a real house before I die, smell lilac in my own garden. If only I could be married again, to Bertie, young enough to be confident, not middle-aged and wary, having seen too much. If only it were Sunday, in summer, just once more, and I were about to take our tea out into the garden. And if only there had been that pram in the hall that is said to stifle all creative endeavour but would have had the opposite effect on me. Our sons, our daughters, playing in that garden, shaking raindrops from those lilac bushes, stalking the cat. Always hot sunshine, in these imaginings. (31–32)

Instead, she sees Sally "Beamish" win her way by "sparkling" at men like Patrick Fox.

Reexamining her life, Blanche thinks that she perhaps need not have engaged in so many "misalliances," been "shackled by the wrong mythology" (108), that she might have struggled in the manner of another classical god, Hercules, whose exploits she looks up and who proves her claim throughout the book: " 'After his death he was held a god, and believed to be the same as the sun.' So the sun *is* God, she thought" (109). She begins to find the courage that will finally let her stop waiting for Bertie's visits and go away on her own, signals that she will get on with her life, by calling Bertie, whom she later imagines "worshipping the sun god" (119), into comparison with Hercules:

What do you do that is so arduous? What have you done today, for example, except to put on that absurd shirt, in Fulham, and drive to the office? Have you been down to Hell and brought back Cerberus on a triple chain? Have you shot the Stymphalian birds? Have you delivered Hesione from the sea monster? Have you *impregnated the fifty daughters of Thespius?* . . . It occurs to me, Bertie, that your life is rather easy, compared with that of Hercules. .... He proves that you can get away with murder and still be admired for it. (110–11; my italics)

And Blanche comes to admire those who "do get away with murder" and to feel sorry for those too "childlike" to try: "She knew now that real pride means gusto; real prive involves fearlessness, bravado, confidence, not a façade behind which one cowers, perplexed, children with a problematic parent they were too inexperienced to challenge. . . . It was, in fact, characters like Sally and like Mousie who had pride, who went into the jungle of human affairs with nothing but their own weapons to defend them" (158).

Besides, *The Misalliance* knows a worse mother than Sally Beamish:

Mrs. Moore, Blanche's own. Blanche shares with Anita Brookner a belief that she never really had a childhood. Had she been allowed to be a child, she might have learned "more winning ways," but her mother was always waiting for her to "grow up and take charge, reminding [her] of onerous duties" (155). Ironically Blanche's mother helped her to begin "her apprenticeship of living alone from an early age" (11). The only child of now-dead parents, whom she claims almost to have forgotten, she is haunted by dreams in which her mother, "a decorative and frivolous woman given to iron requests which brooked no refusal" (68), requires Blanche to row her away from Bertie while Mrs. Duff applauds this act of "obedience."

Blanche's poor relationship with her mother also leads her to the realization that we are as trapped by our dislikes as by our likes. Once again Blanche sees that either-or choices omit all the worlds of possibility in between: disliking her mother, she has tried to be her opposite rather than adopting her mother's best for her own. Thus, Mrs. Moore has influenced her choosing Bertie for a husband: "Her mother was all for Patrick, with his finicky airs and his excellent prospects [though Bertie is the head of a prosperous real estate firm]. Her mother was only too keen for her to avoid entanglements of a distressingly physical nature, which she saw as a direct insult to herself. After all, if Mrs. Moore could manage so well without that kind of thing, why should her daughter not do the same?" (92). Blanche also misses out on a standing social involvement with Barbara and Jack because she cannot play bridge; she refused to learn when her mother kept crying and cheating (19). Blanche's scrupulousness seems to have developed in opposition to Mrs. Moore's lack of scruples and from an inchoate perception that her mother has much in common with the nymphs of the National Gallery and with Sally and Mousie. Blanche traces her lack of female shrewdness to the same source: "All I learnt from my calculating mother was to be her opposite and not to calculate at all" (69). From Mrs. Moore, nonetheless, Blanche has inherited two admonitions that she lives by, though her application is different from what her mother had in mind: "Do it now" (155) and "The best revenge is living well" (46). The latter, unfortunately, merely divides her further from others, for the front she puts up makes her seem remote and uninterested in them. People ignore her because she refuses their pity, and they do not know what else to do for her. Blanche does recognize that one reason she has been so grateful to Bertie is a sense of indebtedness for springing her from "that daughterly trap" (69) and that she has thus willingly assumed the duties of marriage—and more than her share—as a result. In retaliation for the escape Blanche effected, Mrs. Moore "contrived a clever illness" and then "hogged all the attention" at her wedding. Finally acknowledging defeat, she immediately went on a world cruise to find a widower to perform the duties heretofore assigned Blanche.

Patrick too has had his problems with his mother, with whom he has continued to live. When he wants to take Sally away, Blanche questions the honor of doing so by launching into another sermon from Plato: "Honor is the highest good. Pleasure unmixed with reason is apparently what the unenlightened go in for. It does not guarantee a good conscience" (165). He "remonstrates" that he has had "too much of a good conscience" and, having spent years dancing attendance on his widowed mother, has "honored" his parent in accordance with the Ten Commandments. Blanche's response is to imagine that most biblical parents were impossible and that many of the messages in the Bible are "downright subversive" (165), as she also speaks of art (176), additional indications of her individuality and freshness, as well as of why people find her so odd.

Foil Characters

Blanche has the grace to feel guilty particularly about ignoring the overtures of Mrs. Duff, a woman of "eternal commiseration" whose face is "calm and beautiful with concern" (151) and whose only shortcoming is that lack of children. Closer examination, however, suggests certain traits that Blanche finds off-putting, including a tendency to sound as if she has walked out of the pages of Cinderella or some other magnificent womanlore. If Sally is the Sleeping Beauty, for example, Phyllis Duff's "life at home with Mother," a designer of hats and a court milliner, has rather too much of the "charm of a fairy tale" (153). Her husband fell in love with her when she was sixteen, and she made him wait five years until she "judged it seemly" to accept his proposal. He does not know to this day that she had wanted to be a dancer and would have had a career "had it not been for the [first] sight . . . of her future husband, and her determination to marry him, forged in that significant moment" (189). Now the model wife, she freshens up before the good dentist returns home each afternoon and makes the lemon barley water he "swears by" (157). The problem is that even as Blanche reaches back through the "unwieldy furniture in her mind" (13) to pull out the information on Mrs. Duff, the reduction to a type and the phrasing (for example, "modest but superior," though ostensibly of clothes; "my spastics") suggest that she, despite what she says, would not really want to be this woman and that Brookner, more than Blanche, feels some contempt for the type itself. The portrait has the feel of a novelist's preliminary sketch, though we know that Brookner never sets out a program ahead of time:

Phyllis Duff: a good woman. The picture was now clear. Excellent wife, devoted companion. Keeping up to date, up to scratch, planning her wardrobe—modest but superior—with due care but little conceit. Always presentable, in the old fashion of the wife of a professional man, usually to be found in her spotless home. Mrs Duff had no pretensions to be, nor could she ever be mistaken for, the new breed of woman who takes on the world. She had the brilliantly cared for appearance, the fine stockings, the rosy silk scarf, the first-class handbag, of the woman who dresses for a day in town, emerging a little hesitantly from the stony fastness of her mansion flat, looking at all the shops but returning home only with some lampshade trimmings. A woman, in her own and her husband's eyes, of some importance, with sacred rituals: my quiet time, my day for baking, my evening for the League of Friends, my spastics. A woman preserved from another time, smiling trustingly and confidingly, given to pleasantries of a bland and custom-worn nature, lacking in surprises. Blanche reflected on the wholesomeness of Mrs Duff, her extreme remoteness from the world of business activity, from the technological expertise, the sheer boldness, of Bertie's new friend. Like the virtuous woman in the Old Testament, Mrs. Duff supervised all the goings out and the comings in. Her husband, when he left in the morning, knew that when he reached the end of the street, she would be standing at the window or on the little balcony to wave, following him with melancholy brown eyes. And that when he returned in the evening it would be to a warm kiss and the aroma of a serious meal. Blanche . . . imagined Mrs. Duff at her preparations, the gleam of her immaculate kitchen, her gravity, her expertise, her peaceful anticipation of the evening's reunion. Her wifeliness, so out of date, so infinitely beguiling. (13–14)

What Mrs. Duff suggests, to Blanche's amazement, is that women are in control all along: they just have "to know how to handle men, how to make them feel comfortable." After all, "all men were little boys at heart" (189).

Later Blanche feels that if she had only been a Phyllis Duff type instead of "slop[ing] off by her[self], and through shyness bec[oming] quaint" (154), she could have kept Bertie. Her thoughts of Mrs. Duff turn wistful and admiring, turn, we feel, into wishful thinking about herself:

She has that intense femininity that comes from growing up in a woman's world, thought Blanche: a world of confidences, secrets, remedies shared. And it has kept her innocent. She knows nothing of the suspect side of femininity, its conspiratorial aspects, its politics. I am sure that she has never engaged in the sizing up of another woman's chances that disfigures so much female thinking; and I am quite sure she has never done that nasty thing, pretended to be sorry for her women friends in the presence of a man. I am sure that she has never needed to mention another woman to her husband, slyly, to gauge his reaction, because, quite clearly, she is the only woman for him. Philly, he called her. Little Philly, trying on the grown-ups' hats. He probably inherited the name from her mother, and so an unbroken chain of affection has nourished her all through her life. (55)

The problem is that this conclusion is the same as for Mousie (29), and we wonder where Blanche has found the experience on which she draws. Blanche Vernon, though no feminist by any standards, has a quite appealing individuality, which, yielding to the carping of others, she would like to subdue. Again we have the impression that Brookner, rather than Blanche, is speaking, particularly when this keen and satirical eye for the "new woman" or, rather, the "new Mafia" emerges:

It was all the more puzzling in that the baby whom she knew Mousie to be was disguised as a young adult woman who earned her living in an adult way and lunched in wine bars with her young upwardly mobile female friends, all of them busy gentrifying the south-western suburbs and comparing notes on their live-in companions. Marriage they scorned, thinking of it as the shackle that kept women at home, or at best tired out with being too successful all round, yet oaths of fealty were exacted, as in some new code of chivalry. Blanche . . . could see these lunches quite clearly. The talk would be excited, the briefcases parked on an empty chair; acquaintances would be hailed in delighted and uninhibited tones. And when the confidences started, the heads would be lowered and would come together, and the laws of the Mafia would prevail. Mafia honour must be satisfied, no matter what the price to be paid. In fact the price was always survival: No laughing matter, as Blanche had reason to reflect. (29)

Brookner's presence finally becomes conclusive. Blanche may feel that her case is female only, but not Brookner: "She felt herself to be inanimate [a version of "invalid"] and did not know that many people feel like this, men as well as abandoned women" (15).

Miss Elphinstone, another foil for Blanche, could easily have been cut and pasted from a Barbara Pym novel, though Pym's characters are not generally domestics. Brookner even uses one of the tags principally associated with Pym: Miss Elphinstone is an "excellent woman" (86). Like most of the Pym women, she lives—or has the capacity to make Blanche think that she lives—"a lively and dramatic existence . . . in the shadow of some excitable church whose activities absorbed most of her time and whose members abounded in competitive acts of selfless- ness" (22). Like Blanche, she is attentive to her appearance; she has "none of the waistless high-stomached appearance of the elderly" (24) and can smooth and tidy her hair without taking off her hat. The problem is that while Blanche is apparently quite on the up and up in her admiration, we sense that Brookner is not, for Miss Elphinstone turns back, in leaving, to "bare her brilliant false teeth in the sort of smile that betokens an impeccable conscience" (26), and she is "re- tained not so much for her services as for her turn of phrase" (23). Blanche seems oblivious of the satire:

Nothing surprised Miss Elphinstone. Trained in the ways of the Lord, she was proof against all contingencies, although strangely indifferent to life's more savage demonstrations. Routinely cheerful, she could be thought by the un- wary to be complacent, were it not for her smile, which flashed on and off unpredictably; sometimes Blanche would attempt to cut short Miss El- phinstone's elaborate marginalia only to be rewarded by a smile of great benevolence which revealed, if anything, a consciousness greatly superior to her own. Miss Elphinstone, upright and blameless, unchanging in her de- meanour and her attributes, was a tribune of excellence before which Blanche was obliged to lay all her plans. Nothing was really tolerable without Miss Elphinstone's approval. (177)

The problem is that even Blanche is occasionally suspicious of her, if willing to be guided by her. She senses that "for all her propriety, [Miss Elphinstone] sometimes arrived at conclusions which were less than a faint suspicion in Blanche's mind" (86). Again we want to shake Blanche for her gullibility. No one else but her would reach such a conclusion as this:

Miss Elphinstone was demonstrably sane, without fantasies; great was her interest in other lives, yet by some sort of divine sanction she was immune to any effect they might have had on her own. Blanche envied her her impermeability: having no sense of the relative importance or unimportance of others, Miss Elphinstone lived a life of true enlightenment, always mildly

interested but never ill-served by curiosity, and virtuously immune to speculation. (178)

In fact, all around the edges of the reported discourse with Miss Elphinstone, we detect enough gossipy pettiness and pettishness to make
us quite suspicious of both Miss Elphinstone as a person and Blanche as
a reliable narrator. One of the achievements of *The Misalliance* is that
the true domestic of this novel is a male, Mr. Demuth's *homme de
confiance*, Paul, who is effeminate despite being the consort of the virile
Sally and a kind of baby-sitter for Mrs. Demuth.

Every foil, every person on the continuum for Blanche's and our
scrutiny, is quite horribly flawed, to the point that we feel the jaundice
of Brookner's world begin to submerge us. Almost from the opening of
the book, both ends of the continuum merge in the same negation,[6]
another excellent if chilling portrait of old age:

Elderly, tired, and overdressed, the widows of the neighbourhood emerged
from gloomy flats for their afternoon stroll; Blanche saw stark and heavy colour
applied to sagging cheeks and lips, patent leather shoes crammed on to plump
and painful feet, hair golden and unnaturally swirled and groomed. Blanche
watched a woman wearing a heavy fur coat feel for the edge of the pavement
with her stick; a scaly hand, ornamented with long red nails and an accumulation of rings, emerged from the weighty sleeve like a small armadillo. She felt
terror for this woman, as she imagined the painful process of dressing up, of
assembling the attributes of wealthy old age in emblematic and unsympathetic
fashion, much as those nymphs in the National Gallery, with their pearls and
their golden hair, their patrician smiles, had carried their freight of attributes
to mock her present condition. But the nymphs had mocked her own exclusion
from their world of love and pleasure; the widows mocked, like the fates,
unconsciously, indifferently, but with a sense of foreknowledge: you will come
to this. You will be like us, unpartnered, still fashionable, doughty, stiff of
body and sad of mind, obstinate, tough, liable to blame everybody else, our
daughters-in-law who do not telephone us often enough, our grandchildren,
who, although adored, are incomprehensible, the porter of our expensive block
of flats who fails to bring up the laundry, the hairdresser or the manicurist who
plans to take an inconvenient holiday. Blanche, who had neither diamonds nor
fur coats nor daughters-in-law, regarded these women studiously, empathizing
all too accurately with their stoical disappointment. Beneath the golden hair,
their ancient eyes stared back without curiosity, all fellow-feeling long gone,
half-heartedness still whipped up into some sort of discipline, expectations
very low. (10–11)

These are at least widows. Blanche suffers the ignominy of being divorced, and she knows that her only hope for reentering society is by
remarrying; otherwise she will remain "on suspension" (26).

What the novel suggests to us, only to take the proffered solution
away at the penultimate moment in still another display of lacerating
irony, is this alternative: Blanche can "twitch her mantle blue" and get
on with her life, even recognizing her individuality and relishing rather
then lamenting it. In standard Brooknerian fashion, she proclaims her
readiness for change by having her hair cut and by taking up again her
best nightgown, which has been dormant for over a year. But it is also
standard Brooknerian fashion to undermine her new-found independence. She hears a key in the door, and Bertie finally enters her bedroom with "I'm back, Blanche. . . . I've come back. What have you
done to your hair?" (191). That terrible irony is more of a trademark of
Brookner than even the red head (Sally Beamish), the domestic (Miss
Elphinstone), the allusions to painting (for example, Blanche's food as
more worthy of a "still-life painting" than a stomach [99], Paul's being
like Van Gogh's portrait of an actor [134]), the general grayness of
Blanche's world despite her insistence that the "sun is God," the recur-
rence of the word *louche* (101) and of references to Colette (here as the
name of Mr. Demuth's wife) and Henry James[7] (72), as well as other
literary allusions (Blanche's "polished shoes carry[ing] her among well-
trodden ways," [10]), the long suffering of those who must spend
holidays alone (130), the chestnut trees (52), and the leitmotifs or
"mantras" (Paul's "We'll work something out" [144]).

The Novel as Novel

Brookner considers *The Misalliance* "quite different" from her other
novels, "not at all deterministic, and rather sentimental." Pointing out
that it was far better received in the United States, where it was seen as
Jamesian, she suggests the reason and comments on Blanche:

I think they [the English critics] had made the initial mistake of identifying
me with my female protagonists, so that the criticism that comes my way,
particularly in *The Misalliance,* is a semipersonal kind which does not rank as
real criticism: I can't learn from it, I can only feel hurt by it. Also it wasn't a
very good book, but it wasn't *that* bad either. I have written it off. I didn't like
it even as I was writing it. . . .
    . . . [Blanche] was a very aseptic character. The book has quite an interest-

ing theme, which is that even good behavior can go wrong, if it is based on a fallacy or a misconception, that you can't take anything for granted, and that you are walking on egg shells every time you make a choice. . . .
   There is a personal dislike directed against Blanche Vernon, because you can't blame her for anything, except perhaps for being a prig. Now that is a very minor vice in my book. The point is that there are a lot of women like her: nice, innocent, but boring. Nobody likes them and as a result they lead very miserable lives. They are not fun to be with and in England you've got to be *fun;* you must be a *fun* person, having fun all the time! . . . Yet [the novel] is about a moral problem.[8]

In contrast, the achievement of *The Misalliance* is that, for almost the only time since *Hotel du Lac,* the heroine is likable.[9] If Brookner had left her alone at the end, in both senses of the phrase, Blanche Vernon would have been her most successful creation in terms of being transformed by the experience of her novel into a woman of some parts. We like her for making madeira and cherry cakes and for sweating onions for her casseroles; for noting the discrepancy between Sally's grime and poverty and her Le Creuset cookware; for refusing to help Paul smuggle the red fox coat to Sally; for buying the little girl a book on animated trains; for envying women who go to work every day and reading recipe books to find out what they might be having for dinner (99); for thinking of attending the Open University, finishing her thesis, or taking up Cordon Bleu cookery and archaeology (18); and for advising her ex-sister-in-law on the longevity of taramasalata (19). If only Brookner had let her come into an appreciation of her own quaintness as we appreciate it. Again as in *Hotel du Lac,* however, the irony cascades forth. Edith Hope chucks the world all other Brookner women seem to want and lack—marriage—and returns to endure more of the same treatment at the hands of her married lover. Blanche, all set to be her own woman in her own eyes, gets Bertie back, a fate she does not deserve; doubtless, however, she will go on to construe the whole experience as the "fortunate fall." Nonetheless, the structuring is the best yet. We can think back at the end to all the clues and yet still have been struck by the surprise of the true surprise ending.
   The prose is well crafted, with some fetching turns of phrase and descriptions: Blanche "surrounded by a penumbra of vagueness" (103); Sally's "Not with what we've got on the *tapis* at the moment" (120); Blanche, "like many simple women," thinking "in terms of biography" (12); Blanche on Sally: "Perhaps she is really very unhappy and all this

talk is a kind of fugue, a clinical flight from the present" (122); Blanche hearing the rain "crepitating on the leaves of the garden in the early dawn" (114); Blanche's "Where are all the social workers now that we need them?" (125); and the "ragged asters and tight complicated dahlias" that replace "the unconvincing roses and carnations of a metropolitan summer" (179). Again, the point of view is first person masquerading as third, or vice-versa, though we do get inside Patrick's head briefly (95).

Chapter Eight
A Friend from England: "Even in These Liberated Days"

A Member of the Brookner Canon

A Friend from England (1987) is the story of the attachment of loner and "orphan" Rachel Kennedy to the Livingstone family, with whom she is acquainted because Oscar Livingstone was the accountant of her deceased father. One of three partners in a bookshop, Rachel still uses Oscar's services though, having won a significant fortune in the football pools, he has retired from work and now receives her in his home. The Livingstones represent the family life Rachel has never known, and she is drawn to the unit they present, evincing an unconscious envy of the closeness of Oscar, Dorrie, and their daughter Heather but slightly contemptuous of their bourgeois life-style.

Rachel, thirty-two, is an independent woman sworn to be a "plain dealer" and allow no attachments, the legacies of an affair gone wrong. The unworldly family, particularly Dorrie, looks to her to help unworldly Heather, twenty-eight, find her way, but no closeness ever develops between the two women. Moreover, Heather, who is consistently perceived by Rachel to be "shrewd," can make her way quite well on her own, though the man she brings home, Michael Sandberg, along with his overly solicitous father, the "Colonel" or "Teddy," is clearly an incorrect choice from Rachel's (and Oscar's) point of view. They are correct. Rachel finally sees Michael in a wine bar wearing blue eye shadow, lip gloss, and rouge, a vignette for her benefit only. The full story never comes out, but a divorce is efficiently managed, and Michael is dismissed as one who was too much of a child ever to be married.

Rachel quickly ceases to think of Heather as victimized, for she remains in Italy when Dorrie has to have an operation for a lump on an earlobe. Despite the apparent insignificance of the problem, Rachel is appalled that the daughter is not present and recognizes that she is a poor substitute. Only when complications develop and Dorrie nearly dies does Heather answer her father's summons; she is a different sort from Ruth Weiss in *The Debut*. When she reveals that she is returning to Italy immediately to marry an Italian, Rachel is once again horrified at her behavior and has it out with her, confessing the kind of existence she herself leads and urging Heather to renounce her selfishness and live a similarly "pared-down" life (85) near her parents.

Instead Heather convinces her parents, themselves lovers in the highest romantic tradition of literature and opera, that she has found in Marco the love of her life, and they give her their blessing to leave them. When Rachel sees their sadness, particularly that of Dorrie, she vows to go to Venice, despite her hydrophobia, and at least drag Heather back for a visit. The toll her vow exacts is enormous, but she finds time to meet an interesting man on the plane over and to think of calling him while she waits to meet Heather. In the ensuing confrontation, Rachel learns that the confession of the kind of life she leads has only made Heather more determined to have Marco, marriage, children, and the whole traditional romantic package that she has always wanted. She also admits that she has always seen the nicest thing about Rachel as her attachment to Oscar and Dorrie. Rachel returns to London ashamed and defeated. When she meets Oscar in the street several months later, she learns that Heather came home briefly for Dorrie's funeral and that he has sold the house and is going to live abroad. The question that remains for us is whether it was better for the privileged family to have loved and lost or never, like Rachel after that one mistake, to have permitted love at all.

A Friend from England may well take off from this passage in *Providence:* "I [Kitty Maule] am like those awful people who win a large sum on the football pools and swear that it will not change their way of life" (177). Such luck does not change the lives of Oscar and Dorrie—and neither does Rachel. Another first-person narration by the heroine, the novel has a subtexture of jaundiced experience in matters of love similar to that coloring Rachel Kennedy's daily living with eccentricity yet lacks much of the aberration and denial of Frances Hinton in *Look at Me*. Rachel is more forthcoming too, if only for the healthier purpose, as she believes, of setting Heather straight. Brookner has become quite masterful with suspense. Instead of the abrupt revelation of Frances's demeaning relationship, she builds incrementally toward Rachel's "confessing" to Heather in an attempt to make her face her duties to the family:

Listen, Heather, I wanted to get married once. Of course I did. But he was married, and nobody made it easy for me. Yes, I thought like you once. I wanted the same things. But since then. . . . Well, he taught me a lot. He taught me to take care of myself, to give away nothing I couldn't spare. He taught me to see to it that I was the one in control. That's a grim lesson to have to learn. But I learnt it. And I'm still here. And I'm not likely to end up supporting someone else's widowed mother in the back streets of Venice, miles from home. (157)

A Friend from England also enlists suspense and structuring much in the manner of *The Misalliance.* Blanche Vernon, with the loss of Bertie, tries to avoid involvement in the lives of others and ends up being forced to confront the Demuths on behalf of Paul Beamish and, in turn, with the migraine that becomes the climax of the novel. All the way through *A Friend from England,* Rachel not only admits to her hydrophobia but uses water images for her entanglement with the Livingstones (for example, "immersed in the troubled waters of a family drama" [185]). At the end, she must do that which is most repellent to her: go to the "mineral city," Venice, the "ultimate nightmare" (186), to confront Heather.

In one sense, however, the atmosphere of *A Friend from England* has most in common with that of *Family and Friends.* In fact, it would be easy enough to translate the mysterious narrator of the latter into Rachel Kennedy. The bourgeois world both watch in the course of their novels is jeered but also appreciated, and the family bonds are looked at wistfully. Rachel can feel herself "being overtaken by these padded afternoons, these unreal conversations, these respectable bourgeois customs, and the love and comfort that these people offered one another" (24), yet she steadily disavows all "bourgeois sentiments" (131). Though the family under scrutiny in *A Friend from England* is solidly English—as no doubt Brookner means to play on in "Livingstone," as well as "Oscar," "Dorrie," and "Heather"—a mysterious background, reminiscent of that of the Dorns, does hang over the Sandbergs.[1] The middle-class virtues on exhibit in Dorrie and Oscar are more domesticated ones too. The entire family takes a melancholy view of the new-found wealth, as if conscious that it has not been earned: "They seemed to be spending their money more in the line of duty than of pleasure" (16). Oscar "would have been happier working[;] he would have felt ashamed to carry on as before thinking it somehow in keeping to be superannuated now that fate had removed him from the category of

those who need to be seen to earn their money" (17). They do a bit of
remodeling, make purchases for their daughter, particularly for her
wedding, but continue largely unchanged. Dorrie remains as "daintily
houseproud" (13), maintains the same "*reverent* addiction to fine housekeeping" (17; my italics), and still goes to a department store hairdresser rather than finding an elegant salon.

Again the Brookner heroine sees no middle ways. She is on one end
of life's continuum; the Livingstones are on the other. Their "substan-
tial but essentially modest suburban villa" is yet "furnished with volup-
tuous grandeur in approximations of various styles, predominantly
those of several Louis, with late nineteenth- and early twentieth-
century additions" (12). Heather's flat is equally that of a "child of the
middle classes, one who had never known the austerity, the poverty or
the ugliness of an unhappy home. It was also a little out of date, as if
fashions which had come and gone had no purchase here, and only the
solidity of a conventional bourgeois comfort had any meaning" (69).
The accumulated sumptuousness reminds us again of the abodes of
Frances Hinton in *Look at Me* and of the Dorns in *Family and Friends*.[2] It
is in marked contrast to Rachel's deliberately "underfurnished" "small
white bunker" (107) and "unheimlich" flat over the book shop: "a flat
to get out of rather than one to stay in. It was a machine for eating and
sleeping in, a suitable dwelling for a working woman, whose main
interest is in her work. I disliked this version of myself, which seemed
to negate my other activities, reduced them to after-hours amusements,
whereas I had always thought them pretty central" (123). Her life may
lack the "acquisitions" of the Livingstones, but it makes up for such an
absence, she insists, with variety, volatility, and independence (170).

The contrast is not merely in life-style, however. The Livingstones
offer innocence to Rachel's experience—and are "innocent" too in inter-
preting that experience. Rachel attributes her inability to communicate
with Heather to their representing these opposite conditions. The Livingstone family, moreover, is "of great value" to her because "they were
fixed points of reference in a slipping universe, abiding by rules which
everybody else had broken" (31). Their rootedness gives her "the security to be rootless, to test [her] vagrancy against their stability, [her]
preparedness for adventure against their bourgeois world" (67). Ironically they offer "the seduction and the novelty of a fixed point," one
that draws her "on like a charm, perhaps because of the deliberate lack
of fixity in [her] own perspectives" (63).

Rachel also plays off her reality against not simply the Livingstones' lack of reality but romanticism. We distinctly feel that she must reveal the fallaciousness of their view of the world in order to justify her own. She becomes, reluctantly she tries to suggest, the one who dispenses truth and who thus must be, by definition, ill received. A Cassandra figure, she knows that veiling the truth about Heather and Michael's marriage and about the extent of Dorrie's illness is symptomatic of the larger illness, the rose-colored-glasses approach of the Livingstones to life:

Hollow phrases rang in my head, for I was not required to say much in that room [Dorrie's at the clinic] where only compliments and euphemisms were in order. In comparison I seemed to appear to myself as a creature of blunt brute instincts, put into the world in order to point out the facts of the emperor's new clothes: a necessary function but hardly a popular one. And yet I could not reconcile myself to merely being a silent Greek chorus: I was perfectly willing to supply the commentary, but I wanted to have some effect on the action. Unlike the others in that room, I found it enormously difficult to pretend that nothing had happened. These are the facts, I wanted to say; death comes swiftly. And it usually comes too soon, while mourning is endless. Very few can negotiate a stay of execution. The gathering of rosebuds may be recommended, but this is largely a peacetime occupation: for those who have received the warning graver considerations must obtain. I felt like that watchman in the Bible, who is supposed to blow a trumpet when danger approaches, knowing all the time that it is easy to ignore the sound, particularly when it is inconvenient, or when pleasurable expectations are aroused. It is the fate of the watchman not to be heard, but unless he does his job he has no other justification. (165–66)

As usual, the motivations of Brookner's heroine are dim and certainly unexamined by Rachel herself. We infer that the loss of her own parents (as well as the loss of her innocence in that mysterious misalliance in the recent past) has infected her with a need to protect herself by seeing all future possibility as starkly ending in death and disorder. She has no sense that seeing all experience at its worst is as equally flawed as seeing it at its best. Running from the romantics because, we are likely to think, she has not succeeded as a romantic, she takes the opposite stance:

These romantics with their elaborate weddings and their princely trousseaus, and not a thought, or not enough thought, for the sometimes sour and disappointed sensations that follow, as if the world is necessary to sustain the illusion, as if, left alone, no couple can wholly live up to it. This reflection

served the useful function of reaffirming me in my independence, in my
adventurous single state, in my disabused view of human affairs. I would press
ahead with my own enlightened plans. (113)

In fact, she has chosen to live on the surface not only to avoid the
depths but to avoid thought. When, against her better judgment, she
allows her partner, Robin, to get her to go swimming, she is thrown off
balance and made "rather thoughtful for a while":

The process of thinking does not become me. I feel my face growing longer,
my eyes sinking deeper. Thinking, for me, is accompanied by a wave of
sadness. Therefore I try to avoid introspection. I long ago decided to live my
life on the surface, avoiding entanglements, confrontations, situations that
cannot quickly be resolved, friendships that lead to passion. With my quite
interesting work, and the affairs that I keep quiet about, I reckon I manage
pretty well. I tend to be rather merciless with those of my friends who cannot
do the same, and I favour sensible arrangements. I dream a lot, and apart from
my dreams of drowning, I like and value the night hours, when I seem to be in
an altered state. Then I am able to tolerate myself. In the daytime I keep busy,
always on the surface, and that suits me too. Sometimes I meet someone who
makes me think that I might always be as I am in my nocturnal imaginings:
dreamy, vulnerable, childish. The Livingstones fulfilled this function for me.
After being grown-up and liberated throughout the week I could regress
comfortably and safely in their welcoming and uncritical presence. (62–63)

Perhaps the greatest irony of this book is that Rachel, refusing to think
about the consequences of her choices, is virtually oblivious of the merging of physical and nonphysical to which Brookner subjects her. For
example, she is actually an excellent swimmer, for she has grown up on
the coast and gone swimming every morning with her father. What she
has come to fear is "the sight of water," which causes "some vague but
powerful fear of being sucked into it" (61), just as she both fears and is
drawn into the tangle of relations represented by the Livingstones.

Literature and the Romantic Legacy

Where most Brookner heroines fall prey to literature and the romantic
legacy, Rachel pits her reality against the combined biblical and literary
lore that she sees feeding the actions of the Livingstones. Oscar and
Dorrie in particular invest their everyday lives with ritual and ceremony,
and Dorrie is "the virtuous woman in the Bible" (172) once again (along

with, for example, Sofka in *Family and Friends* and Mrs. Duff in *The Misalliance*). Before they became rich, Oscar enacted in his "fairly humdrum circumstances" in Southampton Row "something . . . of a religious office" (9). Tea, though only the family is present, is a ritual. In accusing them of living as though they think that they will live forever, Rachel misses the real truth: the sacramentalizing of the everyday that testifies to their appreciation of it, to their willing of an atmosphere of "a perpetual Sabbath calm" (17). Paradoxically Rachel also feels at times that Oscar and Dorrie, despite inhabiting "a sort of lost paradise of unworldliness," mistrust their luck and see always the skull beneath the skin:

I remembered with astonishment their tranquil investment in the things of this world, as if they thought they were going to live for ever, but at the same time the wistfulness with which they regarded each other, as if they really knew that one of them would die first. What would happen then? Would Heather be up to the task of comforting and sustaining? Would anyone? Who could be a parent to those parents when the time came, when that Biblical day arrived and the silver chord, the golden bowl, revealed their essential fragility? Love, which they had never lacked, surrounded them like a haze of sunlight; they were not made for the dark, as some of us are. Love had made them vulnerable, only able to seek and find each other. And was this condition, which I saw as inherently painful, the reason why their daughter had deliberately chosen its opposite, thus permitting herself to rest secure in the knowledge that she would never suffer abandonment, dereliction, infidelity, bereavement? (79)

At the same time that she is annoyed by the "inherently immovable, or perhaps non-negotiable" about Oscar, Dorrie, and Heather and is particularly annoyed by the last figure, she has "no doubt that in some future incarnation" the parents will "reap the reward promised in the Bible and run to and fro like sparks among the stubble" (29). She sees them acting from a kind of nouveau riche ignorance and, simultaneously, as unchanged by their wealth:

We would all sit down and drink a glass of sherry before Heather and I left: although their sherry was of the highest quality, and the glasses fragile and of a pleasing shape, this ritual was accompanied by an involuntary wince on the part of Oscar and Dorrie. They hated anything sour or sharp, but they confessed to liking the smell of the sherry, which somehow added itself to the vanilla of the cakes and the cigar smoke and the closed-in warmth and

Dorrie's flowery scent. It felt sophisticated to them, and although their standard of comfort was very high they went on adding to it conscientiously, in the same way as they habitually added to Heather's birthright, so that the car, on our return journey, would be packed with parcels, the fruits of a week's shopping on Dorrie's part, for although she looked as if she never left the house, she now recognized the more exclusive department stores as her natural habitat and embarked on a shopping expedition once or twice a week, no doubt with the same expression of resignation that she wore at home. (18–19)

Rachel becomes more biting when she castigates Dorrie for being over-taken, prior to Heather's wedding, by a "fever of spending, a religious ecstasy" (56). She misses the point that, if the Livingstones were trying to effect a style, they would not admit, in her presence, to wincing at the taste of sherry. She also misses the point that however overdone wedding or christening or even funeral preparations and arrangements may be, they make something momentous of everyday matters; they celebrate life and attest to its worth, something denied by Rachel's joyless existing. Her misunderstanding is underscored when she adopts biblical images for herself (for example, the watchman) and particularly when she notes the "supreme irony" of the Livingstones' casting her in the role of the wise virgin (132) but ignores the biblical type for whom she is named, though she knows quite well that Heather is the "prodi-gal" (145) returned and will receive all of his rewards in a reenactment of the age-old drama of life's unfairness.

Rachel also accuses the Livingstones of acting out the inheritance of literature and romance and so gives her author the opportunity to ponder some of her favorites yet again. Their family life is

a distinct culture, rather like the one that had prevailed in the Russian novels I so enjoyed, in which endless days are spent sitting on terraces, and the feckless elder brother worries the nervous married sister and the wan younger daughter is consumed with passion for an unsuitable student, and the retainers enter the drawing-room with the familiarity of long association. I had that same sensa-tion of time being endlessly capacious, and memory and melancholy being equally tyrannical, the sense of strong feeling and deep family commitment, the same insulation from the world, and above all the self-sufficiency. I had no doubt that in her old age Heather would look back on these afternoons with the same sense of loss. What meads, what kvasses were drunk, what pies were baked at Oblomovka! (24)

When the marriage between Michael and Heather is announced, Rachel deems "the festive atmosphere a little too Dickensian in its cheerfulness" and wants to insert her usual "note of realism" (52).[3] She is correct that theirs is a mismatch, but ironically even her famous experience has left her unprepared for the true source of the problem: Michael's homosexuality. She misinterprets, in terms with which she is familiar, his childlikeness, but she has again oversimplified. To her, the world is either adult or child, and, in fact, she equates the entire Livingstone approach to life as being childish. For the family, however, it works, and Dorrie is a particular success:

> She was one of those women who never arrive empty-handed, whose anxious loving care extends to everyone she knows. This great out-flowing of love had been accounted a sign of weakness, of immaturity, by her sharper sisters, who saw her set upon by thieves [another use of biblical imagery by Rachel], spongers, confidence tricksters. But I do not believe that she ever was, thus confounding their expectations. It was they who brought to those tea-parties stories of exploitation by plumbers, shop assistants, traffic wardens, and who went through life in a cloud of suspicion. Dorrie herself was untroubled by all this, and by their forebodings. I suppose she had a charmed life. (87)

What Rachel dismisses as childish could not have existed without a pure type, and Oscar and Dorrie are the genuine article in contradistinction even to the other members of their own family. They prove that the great myths that most of us pursue hopelessly or turn our backs on in sour denial are occasionally reincarnated in the everyday. To Rachel, all this romanticizing of the Livingstones is childish. The only return she can offer for Oscar and Dorrie's hospitality is occasional trips to the theater, ballet, or opera, most often for the light comedies she feels their proper fare, and she is in for a surprise when they attend *La Bohème*, for they hold hands tightly during the last act and blot tears from their eyes. They also prove themselves the genuine article, ordinary people who have discovered positions in the middle of life's continuum: the substance of myth but real flesh. Rachel has to admit that her most persistent image is not just of the Livingstone household but of Oscar's asking after Dorrie when she is momentarily out of his sight. They may be exceptionally loving parents, but their love of their daughter is bound up with how her welfare affects the other mate: "[Oscar] feared for the safety of his daughter because she was in some way responsible for the peace and prosperity of his wife. And Dorrie thought of Heather as not only a loved child but as someone who might cause Oscar to worry. They saw each other exclusively in personal terms" (22). Certainly Dorrie (with perhaps Oscar too) is capable of dying of a broken heart, "that heart they had in common where Heather was concerned," and Rachel comes to see that their story is "from the pages of a nineteenth-century novel" (166). For all her denial, Rachel is just as fatalistic and romantic. She claims to see that Dorrie will die first (80). If she were immune to such fatalism, how would she know to interpret Oscar's constant question ("Where's your mother?") as meaning "so much more than it was designed to mean, as if he feared that the object of his love were eternally about to disappear" (79)? Oscar is not the type to discuss sex or sexual aberrations; he is "only at ease with the noble passions," is moved "by the idea of great and impossible love, the sort of love for which kingdoms were sacrificed, and which might prove to be fatal" (117). In the hospital, Oscar and Dorrie are "returned to their original love dream" (141), and all in the room recognized them as "an enam-oured couple," his kiss on her lips "fervent, exclusive of the rest of us" (140). Rachel can only again connect that fatality with childishness: "There did seem to be a curious sort of dispensation hovering over the two of them, as they held hands like lovers, like children, so deeply attuned to each other that they even breathed in unison" (142). At the tea dance following Heather's marriage, they are able to dance a perfect tango together (recall the short-lived dancing of Betty and Frank in *Family and Friends*). For the lovers, there is no irony in their sense of perfect union, and its absence is what Rachel cannot abide because she can never reachieve a world without irony. She stands not simply in contrast but in opposition:

To me it [romantic passion] was a farrago, both on the stage and in real life, something archaic and unmanageable, unsettling and devastating, and to succumb to such a passion would be a quite voluntary step towards self-destruction. When I thought of those great operatic emotions I felt, for a moment, a quaking, a dissolution, as I had when I surrendered to the drown-ing waters of my dreams. I had no doubt that I would find the real thing as distasteful as I had that commotion, that violent and threatening disturbance that I had experienced when I consented for that one and only time to go with Robin to his health club, and immersed myself, as if fated to try to please him, in those blue and chemical waters. It was a mistake I would not make again. (117)

Like Dorrie and Blanche Vernon of *The Misalliance,* Rachel has had the same "romantic" dream and still occasionally believes in it:

> My own life was spent in the landlocked city streets, which suited me well enough since I had odd fears of death by water. But I looked forward to a time when I would occupy a little house with a garden and have people to tea. I was aware that this was the ambition of a child rather than an adult, and this was rather surprising since, as far as I knew, I behaved in a thoroughly grown-up manner. But obviously some part of me yearned to become suburban again and to hear a garden gate click behind me as I set off on summer evenings to meet my friends. (34)

She may thrust such longings aside on a daily basis, but they haunt her dreams, in which she "bear[s] children, sink[s] smiling into loving arms, fight[s] [her] way out of empty rooms, and regularly drown[s]" (81).

We cannot but wonder, then, why Rachel is so hard on Heather for wanting "from this faintly unlikely match" with Michael "the sort of completeness she had always witnessed in her mother" (47). It is as if Rachel, liking Dorrie and Oscar so much, is almost willing to concede that they are successful romantics. Heather is another matter. She must be like Rachel. Instead she marries once, just to be married (whereas Edith Hope refuses to do so in *Hotel du Lac*), and then claims instantly to have found the love of her life in the romanticized figure of the young Italian, Marco, whom she barely knows. The case is almost more than Rachel can bear. To compound its outrageousness, Oscar and Dorrie are willing to let Heather leave them, albeit with Dorrie sick to her death, and go to him because they want her to have what they have had, and they know that she will have it with Marco: "We saw her face" (183). Dorrie is not the least aware of the need to be embarrassed when she reports that "it's all very romantic. Apparently it was love at first sight" (182), the case with Mrs. Duff in *The Misalliance,* where Blanche, though suspicious, leaves the woman's illusions intact. Cut off from illusion by that unfortunate love affair, Rachel has determined to play the iconoclast; everyone, including her, would be happier if she could put by that compulsion.

Rachel feels that Heather, and the majority of women, are simply in love with the idea of weddings and have gone so far as to develop around them a new—female—"affair of honour": as soon as one woman of one's acquaintance marries, the next one has to follow suit (168).

Again Rachel entirely misses the word play of "affair of honour." A bit
of humor would humanize her considerably. As it is, despite her surface
willingness to function as the eternal wedding guest, to avoid envy, and
never to blame her parents (49), we find her self-serving and have to
remind ourselves to forgive her, for she is, after all, ostensibly in
monologue:

It seemed to me that I conducted my life on rather enlightened principles; that
is to say, I imposed certain restraints on my feelings, kept a very open mind,
rather despised those conventions that are supposed to bring security, and
passed lightly on whenever I saw trouble coming. I had resolved at a very early
stage never to be reduced to any form of emotional beggary, never to plead,
never to impose guilt, and never to consider the world well lost for love. I
think of myself as a plain dealer and I am rather proud of the honesty of my
transactions. After all, I have had to make my way in the world, and I could
only do so by being clear-eyed and self-reliant. I forbid myself to remember
that it has not always been easy, and I never, ever, blame my parents: that sort
of thing is so old hat. I pass lightly through life, without anguished attachments, and this was nearly always the way I intended to be. I say nearly always
because I do sometimes have these odd dreams. (81)

Nonetheless, she constantly gives herself away, as an example, by contrasting the kinds of questions the Livingstones and other parents ask
their daughter with those of her own. Again the contrast is connected
in her mind with children. Because the Kennedys never worried about
her diet, she finds "it so delightful to sit and be fed by Dorrie, whose
food was a magnificent celebration, on an unimaginable scale of magni-
tude, of infant tastes" (22).

Behind her love-hate relationship with the Livingstones is most
likely a sense on Rachel's part that the world, as Margaret Drabble's
characters know very well,[4] belongs to the privileged and that she lacks
the "luck" of entry into that class, though she has many of the trappings (for example, the standard Brooknerian "small legacy" and a
successful line of work). In contrast, Drabble's heroines generally feel
guilty over having everything so easy. Rarely are they among the
nonprivileged, and, when such is the case, as with Clara Maugham in
Jerusalem the Golden, the strain of the struggle takes its toll, as may well
be the situation with Rachel Kennedy:

Someone has to say these things. Someone has to point out to people of
Heather's imperviousness that there are a few duties connected with being an

adult in an adult world. Except that I wished that it did not have to be people like me that issued the warning. I felt the old sickening sense of loss that privileged people always visit on me. It is a peculiar sort of love affair that I have with them. I want to be like them, yet at the same time I want to be taken under their wing, into their protection. And this can never be. For such people know, even before I do, that I am not like them. They are very sorry but the fact is ineluctable. I had seen something of that in Heather's face while I had been trying to bring her to her senses. That look was to return to me frequently in the course of the afternoon. I felt disconsolate and downgraded, but that is sometimes the price one pays for standing one's ground. (159)

Part of the truth, too, is that another Brooknerian heroine is searching for *validity*,[5] a term Rachel uses as she sits in Venice thinking of the coming contest with Heather, which she calls a "tournament," though "not normally given to such romancing" (192). She determines ahead of time to "demystify [Heather], tear down the edifice of this great love which could not stand the light of day but must burrow down through the back streets of Venice, clothed in uniform black" (193). Again we are struck by the convergences in the novel of figurative and literal. Not only has the hydrophobic Rachel condemned Heather's imperturbability and lack of emotion; she describes her as moving through her life "as a swimmer in calm and protected waters, powered only by the healthy movements of a beautifully functioning organism" (28). Now this figure of Heather's great love clothed in black becomes literal: Rachel sees Heather and Marco from a distance, and both are clothed in black. At the tea dance after Heather's marriage to Michael, both bride and groom were dressed in white and looked like children. Rachel's assessment is based on the two ends of the continuum—black to white—but, in either case, marriage is romantic, childish nonsense. We are likely to discredit it all as a severe case of sour grapes.

Women's Matters

Rachel Kennedy cannot be subsumed under such a Barbara Pym tag as "spinster." If not fetching in the way of Edith Hope of *Hotel du Lac* and Blanche Vernon of *The Misalliance,* she is an interesting and unusual psychological type, much in the way of Frances Hinton of *Look at Me.* By her own admission, Rachel is involved in a "hate-love" affair with the Livingstones, and the novel's greatest achievement may be delineating where women are now—at their most knowledgeable, still pulled between the old-style values of fulfillment through marriage and children on the one end of the continuum and the new image of men-denying independents on the other. As ever, we long for more realistic and more productive models in between. When will Brookner, who has fought through her interpretation of writing as a substitute for the "luck" of living and now admits that she enjoys it, give us a woman who has success comparable to her own?

Dorrie introduces her, Rachel thinks "proudly," as "a feminist" (68), and her set thinks Rachel "brave" for enduring such deprivations (77). For her own part, Rachel recognizes that she has given them this impression because of the ease with which she has fallen in with their family entertainments. In all fairness, Rachel, who tends to think of herself as an orphan and a ward, does seem drawn to the family relation-ships and warmth of the Livingstones rather than to the fact of their representing married life. She is entirely alone in the world. Robin can go away to his sister in the country for Christmas even if they do not get along all that well. Rachel is left by herself to mind the store on Christmas Eve. She also knows that, once she buys out the shop, she could, at any point, hang a closed sign on the door and "decamp" with a "ticket to the sun" (much in the anticipated manner of Blanche Vernon in *The Misalliance*). She could make as seamless an exit as anyone, and she knows that many cannot deal with this absence of commitments:

Among my women friends I have noticed one or two wilting under the strain, however brave and resolute they are in pursuit of their own form of fulfillment, the kind we are told to value these days. These are the ones who would secretly have been happier sitting at home listening to Woman's Hour, but instead are to be found on the city streets early in the morning, tapping their way along the pavement in the sort of high-heeled shoes that are supposed to go with attainment, on their way to another day with the computer, or the Stock Exchange prices, or an important presentation, or a client to be exhaustively entertained. And after a day of this they get to meet their friends in a wine bar, where, over a bottle of Frascati, they decide where to go for the evening. Their talk resembles the after-hours conversation of men. "What a day I've had!" they cry to each other. "I'm exhausted! You have no idea how the market is behaving at the moment. I've had New York on the line all day." Bravely they will decide to eat out, although waiters still dislike women diners on their own: they are thought to be a dubious advertisement, spreading the contagion of bad luck around them, not qualifying for the full treatment. Waiters also dislike the plastic swathe of dry cleaning left in the cloakroom, but this has had to be picked up in the lunch hour, otherwise there can be no power dressing for the following day. (170)

It is a trenchantly grand portrait. The only problem is that Rachel should be describing herself and obviously is not; thus, we feel that Brookner is letting off a bit of her own pique about the new woman and at what "we are told to value these days." As usual, the types are extremes: the successful, old-fashioned, one-pair-in-a-lifetime Dorrie and Oscar; those, like Heather, who "set too much store by marriage" (155); those few, like Rachel, who know that Prince Charming does not exist (157); the majority, contrastingly, who, "never entirely lose the faith that it will all come out right in the end, that the next man, or the next, will be the answer to their original expectations of stability and order" (148); those who, like Heather and Ophelia, "turn all to favour and to prettiness" and never tell the harsh truth (175); those who were not born to be married, suffer (as Rachel believes Heather suffers) from "physical mutism," and "exist quite happily in their original child-like state, apparently deaf to the demands of the body (100);[6] those, like Rachel, who avoid love entirely "because they fear its treachery" (105); those, like Rachel, who protect themselves by destroying men; and those, like Heather, who marry the first man who asks them because marriage is not only expected but demanded and continues so "even in these liberated days" (149). In another incisive and scathing portrait of the liberated and the not-liberated woman, Rachel depicts the last two categories in that list. She has about decided not to go away for her usual holiday after the New Year:

Maybe I was getting tired of my way of travelling. I found myself unwilling to take up the burden of providing my friends with amusing anecdotes, largely, I must confess, to persuade them that I was still, as it were, in credit. My friends were rather of the competitive variety, spreading an aura of successful propaganda around their every activity. I suppose most women are like this; at least most of the women I know seem to be. At the heart of their energetic performances—and such woman are not always soothing to be with—lies the desire to persuade others of their great talents in the game of love, their allure, their knowledge, their expertise. Stunning ripostes are theirs, famous scenes are staged, advances are scorned or rejected, new lovers assumed as of right. Circle-like, such women turn men into swine. I do it myself: it is the best protection. It is also rather boring, but the only alternative seems to be something incredibly demanding, for which I am unprepared and for which in any case I do not have the time. And of course yet another alternative is the fate undergone by poor Heather, a pompous and futile marriage, no love, and a lot of embarrassment. (133–34)

The only in-betweens Rachel names are equally flawed and "distasteful": those, like Heather, "who work for fun and marry for status, and still demand compensation" (109). Ironically, among those who do not work at all Rachel cites the courtesans of old (169) and the current "idle women," like Dorrie, whose lives amid their families so fascinate Rachel: "Born to serve, as it might be thought, such women seem to triumph, and many of them preserve a good conscience at the same time. It is quite an achievement" (171).

One reason that Rachel is so negative toward Heather is that the latter has the best of both worlds and does seem to incorporate the span of experience Rachel is depicting. Ever "shrewd" (Rachel's principal tag for her), Heather enacts the "emancipated image" that her parents imagine her to desire (15) and merely uses it to keep her own counsel and go her own way while acting the good daughter on all requisite occasions. Again we are struck by the apparent inability of Rachel to take more sophisticated readings of character (or experience). She alternates between railing at Heather for her shrewdness and for her malleability and converting the latter into evidence against her, as the figurative is so often converted in this book, to physicality. Thus Heather's "bovine expression" (65) does not change at all throughout the marriage with Michael: "One thought of her not exactly as a woman but as some sort of animal known for its unassuming qualities, a heifer, perhaps. Heifers are also traditionally associated with sacrifice. The difficulty with Heather seemed to be that she lacked the emotional equipment even for sacrifice, though sacrifices were planned for her by those watchful aunts" (29).

Not understanding, either, the real problem with Michael, Rachel is ready to blame the obvious failure of the marriage on sexual incompatibility brought on, probably, by the interference of Oscar and Dorrie and their reconstruction of the bridal flat in the image of their home, though with an icy blue master bedroom that prohibits contact. Rachel hints at something unhealthy in the relation between father and daughter (a recurrent notion in Brookner that reminds us here of Rachel's own phobia about swimming, originally enjoyed with the father), for Oscar has given Heather a kitten on which she lavishes her affection rather than Michael, and the key that Rachel hears in Heather's door is not the husband's but the father's.[7] She also imagines him "a suppliant, with

his roses, outside his daughter's door" (76). Rachel is willing to blame
Heather for her lack of tolerance; maybe Michael is not "the world's
most exciting man," but many women would envy her situation (109).
Then, hardly past the honeymoon-divorce, Heather is off again without
penance; Rachel is outraged once more. The least she could do is
"inaugurate a period of official spinsterhood" until the time is more
"propitious" for her to renounce her parents and announce Marco (152).
She will be the eternal victim all over again:

> She would become one of those efficient women in the rag trade, disaffectedly
> reviewing fashions, looked on for tips to current trends. Time and age would
> happen to her, bulking out her already sturdy figure, fading her hair, and the
> vision still far off, waiting to be sought. I could see her in her parents'
> drawing-room in years to come, a little untidy round the hips, a little weary,
> still polite, still private, as she tended their now wistful expectations, parrying
> their questions, giving no hint. It was no life for a decent woman, and yet it is
> the life that many women have had to lead. And it is the lot of such women to
> be despised, as if they had failed some essential test, the test that more
> fortunate women have had the wit to pass. No sign of love would appear to
> change that changeless expression, and eventually she would find herself indis-
> pensable to her friends, as reflector, as recipient of confidences, as baby-sitter,
> as flavour enhancer of safer and more recognized conditions. No amount of
> transient lovers would redeem her status. She would be referred to as "poor
> Heather." And women of a more conventional stripe would feel gloriously
> sorry for her. (148–49)

Rachel seems to sense in Heather a rival. Increasingly she has had to
be the daughter's stand-in with Dorrie and Oscar. Now, with Marco
and the possibilities he opens up, Heather is "usurping" Rachel's "independence," using her time "to enjoy the equivalent" of Rachel's "habitual adventures" (148). This supposedly conventional woman, whom
Rachel was to have educated in the ways of the world, is fast outstrip-
ping the would-be teacher. What Rachel is most upset about is the fact
that the fortunate few "get it all": marriage (Michael) and romantic
adventure (Marco). Never mind that both relationships are far from
perfect, that, in the latter, for example, is the very unromantic Italian
mother to be cared for.

Men-women relationships are not the only cause for Rachel Kennedy's retreat from human connection, however. As has been suggested, a muted but persistent theme is the haunting fear of mortality:
"the additional curse of happy families . . . was to fear the loss of one of

its members, to be unmanned by every accident that could befall a child or a husband or a mother" (131). At least the person who lives alone has to think only of his or her own extinction. We infer that Rachel's relation with her parents ("all the illnesses I had endured") has led her to this stance and that she has reacted to the lingering death of her mother, reinvoked by the sight of Dorrie in the clinic and at the verge of death. We note the conflation of images and themes. The glimpse she has of Dorrie makes her look "as if she were drowning," and the whole episode returns Rachel to her childhood (162). When "such sieges and fugues"[8] overtake her, she dresses up and plies her standard tool of distraction: "I go out, seek companions, bear them home. I live on the surface, plunging ahead, attached only to the present, with only a wary eye to the future. No bourgeois sentiments for me, no noble passions. The surface, the surface only" (131). While the loss of parents has supposedly made Rachel more self-reliant and therefore more reliable as a model for Heather, Rachel does know the cost, and it is not only the isolation from others; the standard necessity of a Brookner heroine to fill time, often by roaming the streets; or the requirements levied by living alone successfully: "it is probably necessary to have an audience [the case of Frances in Look at Me], or else to be so steeped in self-esteem that one's every action is perceived as ceremonious [the case with no Brookner heroine]" (26). A major hazard is that the liberated woman is considered "fair game" (81), and Rachel does not seem to understand her full victimization when she flees her flat and walks in the evenings to ensure not being in when Teddy Sandberg calls her. She does not notice the oxymoronic overlay of her escape into the "landlocked freedom" of the streets (82). Again she lives by absolutes—"Whatever women put up with from men, they should never countenance indifference" (118); "The true adventuress knows that she can never go home again" (149)—that offer little hope of real self-examination, however meticulously self-examining she thinks she is.

Finally, as is so often the case, Brookner undercuts her heroine's stances. On the one hand, though we do not get inside his head, we see in Robin a physical division that is a foil for Rachel's contrast of surface and inner lives. The male loner can suffer as much as the female, as Brookner doubtless means to remind us when she has Rachel select this "male" image: standing in for Heather with Oscar and Dorrie, she feels "like the reserve in some key football match" (141), a reminder, too, of the source of the Livingstones' wealth.[9] He "copes with his life extremely well by belonging to a lot of clubs" and finding new wine bars. He claims never to be lonely in a London that satisfies all of his needs, but he still takes "package art tours of Italy or walks" for his vacations (60). He dresses "like a poor clerk in the daytime and a man about town in the evenings": "after his evening swim he would want to change his personality; the working day would thus be symbolically washed away, and the real, the authentic Robin would emerge, as if after a baptism" (83). Refusing to swim, Rachel shuts herself off from the hope of real change while pretending that the genesis of the surface life she leads away from those who know her is real change. What we cannot understand is why Robin and Rachel do not make a couple, as Dorrie believes them to be when she comes to the book store. More surprising is the fact that Rachel never raises the issue even by way of conjecturing about Robin's sexual preferences. They are, after all, close. He is the only one who knows about her fear of water, and he cares for her when she is ill. She has taken Heather to task for being intolerant of the unexciting Michael, but nothing condemning emerges about Robin at all. He simply seems another confirmation of Rachel's obtuseness, with Rachel a female version, like Ruth Weiss in *The Debut,* of John Marcher in Henry James's "The Beast in the Jungle," though she lacks Ruth's passivity.

The most telling and ironic puncturing of the elaborate structure that Rachel has framed for her life, however, occurs in Venice, that city of nightmare for her, and occurs, fittingly again for her creator, through art.[10] Killing time until she can confront Heather, she forces herself to go to the Accademia for the one picture that she wants to see, one that combines motherhood and the mysterious male figure, the knight:

Bellini's Madonnas turned cheeks shadowed with sorrow in my direction, their heads describing an arc of grief which nevertheless excluded my inheritance. In a deserted room I found the only picture I wanted to see. The woman suckling her child had a heavy face, immanent with meaning, but from which all explanation had been withdrawn. To her right, on the left of the picture, stood the mysterious and elegant knight, intense and remote, his face in shadow. The storm that broke on the scene bound the two together in puzzling complicity. In the background, a banal hill village. In the middle distance, two broken columns. (191)

Later, Heather's face will seem "to have the same moody distant expression as the woman suckling her baby" in that picture (201). Heather,

who is so beneath Rachel's contempt as to have "temperament" rather
than "personality" and who is "above all at home with materiality"
(20), continues to have it all:

She would, once again, have the status of a married woman, a condition which
a person as conventional as herself would consider indispensable. She might
even have the great love she claimed as hers. Eventually she would have
children, would bring them home for a visit, and be acclaimed, simply for the
fact of having passed the essential test. For that is the test, make no mistake
about it. (200)

Rachel, in contrast, sees that the life she has fabricated is not enough:

The fact of the matter was that the wonders of this earth suddenly meant
nothing to me. Without a face opposite mine the world was empty; without
another voice it was silent. I foresaw a future in which I would always eat too
early, the first guest in empty restaurants, after which I would go to bed too
early and get up too early, anxious to begin another day in order that it might
soon be ended. I lacked the patience or the confidence to invent a life for
myself, and would always be dependent on the lives of others. (204)

While the novel is far from sanguine, Rachel, in contradistinction to
most other Brookner heroines, has learned; the rest usually see with
certainty the futures of others.

The Novel as Novel

Rachel makes a larger mistake in her assessment of Heather and the
Livingstones than former Brookner heroines (for example, Kitty in
Providence about the relationship between Maurice and "Miss Fairchild"), but we may not care as much. We are given the same careful
analysis of character, insofar as we can trust the first-person narrator,
but even less of a plot than in the previous novels. More prominent
than usual is the tendency of the characters to overdramatize their lives
by expecting apotheoses (13, 116).

The word power here is evident in, for example, "the high-octane
accessibility" (144) of Michael and his father and in the stark and rare
symbols, as when Rachel, going again to the Livingstones after Dorrie's
supposed recovery, finds change: "The house, as I stood outside it,
seemed smaller than I had remembered, and the garden less immaculate: one drowned rose hung limply from its stem" (179). The

"drowned rose" is Dorrie, who will die from what is apparently the cancer that had seemed merely a wen on an ear, but the metaphor, as simple as it is, enlarges to the whole presentation of Rachel, with her Cassandra-like fixation on the truth no one wants to hear or believe and her fear of water that forecasts her own drowning in the lives of those she has meant to distance. Moreover, for those familiar with Brookner's other novels, Rachel's going on to describe Dorrie's doing her hair in a new way to hide her damaged earlobe ironically forecasts sad consequences rather than renewal.

Other standard Brookner fare is here too, though with some thoughtful variations. The leitmotif is Dorrie's "I hope I did the right thing" (22), but it truly defines her unassuming nature and speaks again to the world of bourgeois values from which Rachel would cut herself off. The chestnuts are present (89), but their accustomed image of breaking from the shell, as well as their color, has been usurped: Heather wears not only a chestnut suit but moccasins "the colour of conkers when they first split the green husk and emerge, glistening, to lie among the fallen leaves" (32). As has been suggested, however, perhaps the most interesting feature of *A Friend from England* is the interlacing symbiosis of literal and figurative in ways that reflect negatively on a heroine who constantly delineates experience in terms of extremes and opposites. In Venice, for example, she sees a child chasing a ball and, when his mother calls him "Marco," interprets the generic as a sign, since she has come there to lure Heather away from her Italian lover of that name. When Heather says that Marco wants nothing to do with Rachel, she can only admonish Heather for not passing her off as just "a friend from England" (202) after stoutly denying throughout the book that they have ever been friends. Until this point at the end, we may not have known just how ironic the title of the novel actually was, particularly when Heather immediately makes clear that her relationship with Marco is already verging on the closeness of that of her parents: "I tell him everything, you see" (202). Who is the plain dealer now, and in how different a way? The Italian male is much closer than the female friend from England, who, again in standard Brooknerian form, is not very "English" herself. Worse, the "plain dealer" has been reduced to wishing for a lie.

The overwhelming effect of *A Friend from England* remains the conflation of image and idea: children and childhood, drowning literally and figuratively. The fact that nothing is ever made of all this is testimony to the lack of clarity masked by Rachel's adoption of absolutes. She wants the childhood that has been denied her and to some extent tries to relive it by becoming the willing substitute for Heather in the bosom of the Livingstone family. In turn, she cannot fully condemn Michael because she understands that his life is a way of seeking revenge for his own "spoilt childhood" (144) and sees that his father is actually the most victimized of them all, having been goaded first into providing "a cover for this incorrigible child, so that he might enjoy his little games under the cloak of respectability" (116). She accuses others—those "normal" like Dorrie and Oscar—of living for the extremes (for example, "Until then, between the wedding and the christening, so to speak, they were in abeyance" [90]) but is oblivious of a similar kind of diminution of experience on her part. It is almost as if she can remake reality by her own choice of images. Hating water, she yet applies it figuratively to all experience, thinking of herself as "drifting" on the "stream" of the Livingstones' talk, annihilating her own complexity and theirs: "From their withdrawn expressions I assumed them to be living at some subterranean level, immersed in a sea-dream that never rose to the surface. Their sleepwalking demeanour, the food that always appeared as if by magic, and the abundance of material goods that flowed through their lives I took to be signs of a fortunate dispensation" (63–64). Away from them, she feels herself adrift.

Brookner, always rather eccentric in conception and perception, seems increasingly to combine the sardonic and the whimsical. The use of water in A Friend from England is a case in point. The gray of most of the other novels yields here to a persistent rain and to water rushing from a broken pipe; to a hydrophobia that "darkens the edges" of the heroine's mind (153); to Rachel's inability to stand the sight of Robin pouring a glass of water down his throat (153); to Venice; and, all the way through, to the connecting of virtually all human emotions with "the drowning waters" of dreams (117). Suddenly the high seriousness latent in such an atmosphere is shattered by the fact that the wine bar in which Michael stands revealed to Rachel is decorated like an ocean liner, though underground, and is in fact named the "Titanic." The standard golden figure (a dog in Family and Friends) recurs in this novel but is not one of the rich. Rather it is Michael, "the ruined child" (75): "His main feature was his hair: conspicuously golden, thick and wavy, hair that is rarely seen on a man once he has passed adolescence" (43). What are we to make of the nexus? Both he and Heather are persistently described in images of children and childhood, as are the Livingstones and their romanticizing, and Rachel is both drawn and repelled as if somehow to reclaim her childhood through them would set her life right. Their wedding dance, surrounded by a veil of water, is a children's party to which Rachel goes with shoes in a paper bag as if she were indeed a child attending a party (57). At it, bride and groom are like children learning to dance at a dancing school to a wind-up gramophone "while the rain streamed down and drowned all the white flowers" (58–59). Rachel both regresses with the couple and the whole Livingstone family into childhood and chides herself and them for doing so.

Here is Brookner's own summary of *A Friend from England,* which she finds "a very old-fashioned moral tale":

It is about an extremely emancipated young woman—whom they will *not* be able to think is me!—who is drawn into a family of blameless innocence whom she feels called upon to protect, but by whose innocence she finds herself finally vanquished. She can't measure up to it. It is quite complicated, not only because it has a larger cast but because it is about men.[11]

In fact, *A Friend from England* hardly seems old-fashioned at all.

Chapter Nine
The Achievement of Anita Brookner

Anita Brookner has had/has three careers: don, art historian, and novelist. As much as anyone else we might think of, she suggests that learning and creativity never have to stop. Who else has had a first novel published at age fifty-three and gone on to become not only one of the most prolific but one of the most well-recognized craftsmen of the time? Who else, for that matter, reads not only literature but *contemporary* literature with such avidity and such fairness and even purchases hard bound versions to help out her fellow writers (accompanied when she admitted it, doubtless, with the proverbial twinkling eye)? She has left teaching and will not again write art criticism, but her mark is on her professional field. As we have seen, her book on David is accounted a model of its genre. Finally, as the first woman to hold the title of Slade Professor at Cambridge, Dr. Brookner has modeled in another way as well.

Anita Brookner has been both a popular and a critical success as a novelist, though some detractors have seemed to confuse her as an author with her own creation, romance novelist Edith Hope in *Hotel du Lac*. She has put learning and allusion and crafted prose back into vogue while denying that she is much of a craftsman at all. Her novels, she claims, just happen out of her questioning: if this or that is the problem, how will the protagonist react, what are the choices (mostly) she has, and which will she pick? Her first novel, *A Start in Life,* was an immediate success with critics and the reading public. The fourth, *Hotel du Lac,* won the 1984 Booker-McConnell Prize and was filmed for television in 1986.

Brookner has also reintroduced us to moral choice and reminded us of the novel's genuine legacy as a purveyor of values. Like Margaret Drabble, she knows how much we have abused the privilege and how often we, with their heroines, misuse literature and the popularized versions of women and men (and the relations between them) we deem literary.

Brookner's novels, except for *Hotel du Lac* and *The Misalliance,* are not comfortable reading. Something is going on in her books that is beyond comfort. We come away from them in internal debate. We have to think, if only to disagree. We may not know exactly what has happened; she does not always seem to know. Nothing much may have happened at all except at the level of inner (deep inner) landscape. When we stop to think, though, we realize the feat: she has taken us, through one (sometimes very small) human psyche, across hecatombs (a word she likes) of human reach—pagan, Christian (though she is Jewish), female, male, principled, unprincipled. She has made the trek without being licentious or bawdy, deceitful or euphemistic. Particularly for our time, she is quite unusual.

Notes and References

Chapter One

1. So Brookner indicates in a letter to the author dated 2 August, 1988.
2. Brookner's love affairs are reported in Annie Roston, *"Look at Me,"* *Harper's* (July 1983), 75. However, I am indebted for most of the facts about and views of Anita Brookner to the interview of Shusha Guppy, "The Art of Fiction XCVIII: Anita Brookner," *Paris Review* 29 (1987), 147–69. An example of the biographical problems connected with Brookner is the confusion about her date of birth, which is listed as 1938 in such standard sources as *Contemporary Authors, Contemporary Literary Criticism,* and *Who's Who 1984,* but is actually 1928, as claimed in *Who's Who 1974* and verified by Dr. Brookner (in a letter to the author dated 16 August, 1988). As a result, she has been thought to have started publishing novels when she was in her mid-forties, a feat unusual enough. Actually, however, she was fifty-three the year that the first novel came out.
3. Margaret Drabble, *A Writer's Britain: Landscape in Literature* (New York, 1979), 7.
4. Joyce Carol Oates, "Bricks and Mortar," *Ms.* (August 1974), 35.
5. *The Misalliance* (New York, 1986), 26–27. Subsequent references, cited parenthetically in the text, are to this edition. For Brookner's other novels, the following editions are used: *The Debut* (New York, 1981); *Providence* (New York, 1982); *Look at Me* (New York, 1983); *Hotel du Lac* (New York, 1984); *Family and Friends* (New York, 1985); *A Friend from England* (New York, 1987).
6. Guppy, "Art of Fiction," p. 149.
7. Ibid.
8. Ibid., p. 150.
9. Merle Rubin, "Casting Moral Puzzles: A Novelist on Her Craft," *Christian Science Monitor,* 1 March 1985, B3. Based on a telephone interview with Brookner.
10. Guppy, "Art of Fiction," p. 149.
11. Ibid., p. 168.
12. Anita Brookner, "The Bibliothèque Nationale," *Times Literary Supplement,* 5 October 1984, 26.
13. Guppy, "Art of Fiction," p. 148, describes her as follows: "She . . . look[s] very feminine: petite, slim, and casually but most elegantly dressed. Reddish well-cut hair frames her pale, striking face, which is dominated by large beautiful blue eyes. Her exquisite manners disarm and put visitors at

ease, and at the same time secure a reasonable distance. She speaks in a deep, gentle voice, with fluency and deliberation in equal measure, and sometimes in 'short, military sentences,' as she once said of Stendhal. Occasionally she smokes a very slim cigarette."

14. Brookner, "The Bibliothèque Nationale."

15. Guppy, "Art of Fiction," p. 168.

16. Ibid., p. 169.

17. Described in ibid., 149, 152–53, 156–60, 165, 167–68.

18. In Rubin, "Casting Moral Puzzles," Brookner says that she most admires among novelists "Dickens, above all. And all the great moralists. And Henry James, certainly."

19. See ibid.

20. Guppy, "Art of Fiction." p. 163.

21. Ibid.

22. Ibid., p. 164.

23. Ibid., 168.

24. Ibid., 150–51.

25. Ibid., 148.

26. Brookner's comments on her writing style are drawn from ibid., 162–65.

Chapter Two

1. Mary Anne Schofield, in "Spinster's Fare: Rites of Passage in Anita Brookner's Fiction," *Cooking by the Book: Food in Literature and Culture,* ed. Schofield (Bowling Green, Ohio: Popular Culture Press, in press), has an excellent account of Ruth's initiation into adulthood, as conveyed in food imagery and discussions of food in *The Debut,* though she is much more sanguine than I am about the growth that takes place in Ruth.

2. The description is from Guppy, "Art of Fiction," 150, who sees Brookner's males as deliberately contrasting with the "foreignness" of her heroines. Brookner finds the contrast "more between damaged people and those who are undamaged."

3. In Brookner's latest novel, *A Friend from England,* the heroine, Rachel Kennedy, owns a bookstore, though it does not deal only in rare books.

4. *A Start in Life* or *The Debut* takes its title from Balzac's novel, *Un Début dans la vie,* which is one of the *Scènes de la vie privée* of Balzac's *Comédie humaine.* Brooker may well have had in mind, too, playing on the fact that it is her debut as a fiction writer.

5. A statement by Brookner in Guppy, "Art of Fiction," 149.

6. Brookner's father loved Dickens and "thought Dickens gave a true picture of England, where right always triumphed." Brookner reads a Dickens novel every year and is "still looking for a Nicholas Nickleby!" (ibid., 149). He is frequently mentioned in her novels.

7. Here is Brookner's way of accounting for why Anna Karenina fails: "Anna loses because, for all her boldness, she can't commit herself morally to her actions. She feels guilty about her son and misjudges her Vronsky. She can't accept that men can't keep up the same pitch of passion as women can—that they cool off. With men passion is all at the beginning and with women it is all along." Ibid., 152–53.

8. Brookner proclaims *The Debut* very autobiographical: "I wrote it in a moment of sadness and desperation. My life seemed to be drifting in predictable channels and I wanted to know how I deserved such a fate. I thought if I could write about it I would be able to impose some structure on my experience. It gave me a feeling of being at least in control. It was an exercise in self-analysis, and I tried to make it as objective as possible [a constant aim of Flaubert]—no self-pity and no self-justification. But what is interesting about self-analysis is that it leads nowhere—it is an art form in itself" (Guppy, "Art of Fiction," 150–51), a rather exact rendering of Ruth's case in *The Debut*.

9. The merging of literal and figurative (for example, food here and drowning in *A Friend from England*) is a strong motif in Brookner's fiction.

10. Introduction (anonymous), "Anita Brookner: *Hotel du Lac*." *Contemporary Literary Criticism Yearbook* 34 (1984), 136.

11. Guppy, "Art of Fiction," 148.

12. Brookner had "fragile" health when she was growing up and was thus not permitted to learn Hebrew. Ibid., 149.

13. Brookner "prefer[s] the company of men because they teach [her] things [she doesn't] know." She agrees with Sartre that "L'homme c'est l'autre": "It is the otherness that fascinates me." Ibid., 161.

14. According to Annie Gottlieb, "the chilling portrait of Ruth's deliquescent mother is right out of Christiana Stead." "Three Hapless Heroines," *New York Times Book Review*, 29 March 1981, 14.

Chapter Three

1. As in *The Debut*, Brookner also justifies the autobiographical in fiction. Kitty tells her students "that in this period fiction, indeed all creative endeavour, becomes permeated with the author's own autobiography" (130).

2. Brookner may be thinking, in different terms, of her own spiritual struggles. She "would like to be able to join in [Judaism] fully. Not that [she is] a believer, but [she] would like to be." Guppy, "Art of Fiction," 149–50.

3. Most of Brookner's novels deal to some extent with the father-daughter relation.

4. Responding to her interviewer's question about this stance in *Providence* as having to do with style, Brookner says: "I am not conscious of having a style. I write quite easily, without thinking about the words much but rather about what they want to say. I do think that respect for form is absolutely necessary in any art form—painting, writing, anything. I try to write as

lucidly as possible. You might say that lucidity is a conscious preoccupation."
Guppy, "Art of Fiction," 162–63. Extracting, then, we are likely to conclude
that one of Kitty's problems is the inability to move beyond individual words
to what they mean to say and to the form in which they are said and out of
which they come.

5. Rubin, "Casting Moral Puzzles," sees an ironic play on "pro-vidence"
or "foresight" in the title.

6. Jane is the other end of the continuum of women that dominates all
of the Brookner novels; those in her class are so beautiful or so bold or so
demanding that they pull all in their wake by simply existing. What we have a
hard time accepting is that the heroines—at the other end of the continuum—
do not make more of themselves. They are not, as the continuum would lead
us to suspect, ugly, simply too unassertive and too unwilling to use what they
have. Brookner is, of course, having fun with the names here. Jane is no "plain
Jane" but a "fair child." Maurice "Bishop" has a strong religious bent, though
we may think that it, too, is posturing.

7. See Judith Gies, "An Anachronism in Love," *New York Times Book
Review*, 18 March 1984, 17: "Superficially, all this genteel ado sounds much
like Barbara Pym territory, and there is much here that is similar—wit,
detachment, gentle spinsters. But Miss Brookner's work is more ambitious
and more disturbing. Barbara Pym's women belong in a context. When men
disappoint (as they invariably do), there are always the comforts of the parish
jumble sale. Kitty Maule, on the other hand, is an anachronism, and we sense
that her future will not be cozy."

8. Kitty, the expert on the romantics, never seems to consider that, as
Brookner points out: "The Romantics tried to compensate for the absence of
God with furious creative activity. If you do not have the gift of faith which
wraps everything up in a foolproof system and which is predicated on the belief
that there is a loving Father who will do the best for you, then, as Sartre said,
you have to live out of that system completely, and become your own father."
Guppy, "Art of Fiction," 154. She also interprets Maurice, a nonromantic by
these terms, as a romantic.

9. Ibid., 158.

10. Ibid., 153.

11. Answering the query of why existentialism, a seeming opposite of
determinism, is the only philosophy she can endorse, Brookner says: "I don't
believe that anyone is free. What I meant was that existentialism is about
being a saint without God; being your own hero, without all the sanction and
support of religion or society. Freedom in existentialist terms breeds anxiety,
and you have to accept that anxiety as the price to pay. I think choice is a
luxury most people can't afford. I mean when you make a break for freedom
you don't necessarily find company on the way, you find loneliness. Life is a
pilgrimage and if you don't play by the rules you don't find the Road to

Damascus, you find the Crown of Thorn [*sic*]." Ibid., 153–54. The only problem is that Kitty plays by the rules, at least insofar as she knows the rules, and still gets the Crown of Thorns.

12. It is interesting to recall, in this regard, that the name of Margaret Drabble's ninth novel was *The Middle Ground.*

13. Guppy, "Art of Fiction," 152.

14. Brookner may have been remembering Wordsworth's "Lucy poems" when she named Maurice's lost love.

15. Alfred Hitchcock came to be known for making a brief appearance in each of his films. Similarly, Brookner seems to remember her own reddish hair in at least one character per novel (with *A Friend from England* seemingly the one exception).

16. Brookner lets her characters assess others in shocking statements, even if they are meant to be private observations. We wonder how Caroline can be a friend but a stupid one or how Heather in *A Friend from England,* also ostensibly a friend, can be described by Rachel as so bovine. A number of critics have commented on how condescending Brookner's heroines are.

17. According to Gies, "Anachronism in Love," 17, Kitty's "thoughts on the fate of Dante's Paolo and Francesca reflect a tragicomic ambivalence toward the moral standards and the expectations we learn from books, an ambivalence she shares with the protagonists of" *The Debut* and *Look at Me.*

18. The passage forecasts the arguments Sofka will use to persuade her daughter Mimi to marry old Lautner in *Family and Friends.* Gies finds Kitty herself a type: "Kitty's plight sometimes seems metaphorical, and Kitty herself not so much a real woman as a symbol of the disappointed child in all of us." Ibid., 17.

19. Guppy, "Art of Fiction," 152.

20. The term was coined by Kenneith Calvert of the Department of Education of Georgia College.

21. See Marion Glastonbury, "Sentimental Education," *New Statesman,* 14 May 1982, 25: "[the] portraits of age—the ailing couturière, and the blind invalid who was once a philosophy don—are genuinely poignant. When the young suffer disappointment, the old are cheated of the vicarious fulfillment they feel entitled to expect."

22. See Schofield, "Spinster's Fare," who believes that the references to food demark Kitty's "growing up," finding a "new language," and being "initiated to herself." In contrast, I think Kitty has simply learned to settle for half a loaf when she does not have to.

Chapter Four

1. Brookner suggests that "they [the American publishers] thought *Providence* too 'downbeat.' " Cited by Rubin, "Casting Moral Puzzles."

2. Diminutives are generally disliked in Brookner novels. As examples, Sofka's reducing her daughters to "Mimi" and "Betty" is satirized; and Michael, who never fits in, "cannibalizes" Heather's name to "Hetty" in *A Friend from England* (54).

3. Mary Cantwell, "Not Hungry Enough," *New York Times Book Review,* 22 May 1983, 14.

4. Brookner may draw on John Mortimer's epithet for Rumpole's wife, Hilda. Humor is not a frequent tool of Brookner in the early novels, but she perhaps enlists it in *Look at Me* because Frances claims that she makes her readers laugh. Examples are Nick's describing Maria as "Italy's very own nuclear warhead" (35) and Frances seeing that Nick's "effect on women measured something very high on the Richter scale" (37), with possibly a "naughty" pun on "rictus."

5. Brookner's comments appear in Guppy, "Art of Fiction," 151–52. He adds: "You say, in *Providence,* that you write to tell the truth, what you call the Cassandra complex," a view that becomes a veritable compulsion for Rachel Kennedy in *A Friend from England,* though she is not a writer. Brookner tells Guppy that "we all try to put some order into chaos. The truth I'm trying to convey is not a startling one, it is simply a peeling away of affectation. I use whatever gift I have to get behind the façade."

6. Anne Duchêne, "Superior Melancholy," *Times Literary Supplement,* 25 March 1983, 289.

7. Her career as an art historian gets some play too as she describes artists' depictions of melancholy and madness (e.g., 6–8).

8. Cf. Stephen Harvey, "*Look at Me,*" *Village Voice,* 5 July 1983, 46: "But Frances's dreariest fate, if she only realized it, is to be trapped inside her own precious, suffocating self. . . . And since she is the narrator/protagonist of this introverted book, the hapless reader is trapped right along with her. Frances characterizes herself as a self-effacing observer, who longs to act and be noticed. 'I needed to learn, from experts,' she sighs, 'that pure egotism that had always escaped me'; if you ask me Frances does just fine in that department on her own. Rarely has a novel been so cluttered with the first-person-singular-pronoun; Frances's 'I' appears 34 times on p. 123 alone."

9. As we have seen, Brookner likes the term *viable.* She uses it serio-comically in *Providence.* Robert Taubman ("Submission," *London Review of Books,* 20 May–2 June 1982, 18) sees Kitty in that novel as "the sort of heroine an author invents to subject her to a life of disappointments [that] are mitigated for her by academic interests" and by the fact that "the novel is warm and delightful about donnish life, exhibiting its own kind of donnishness in a sentence like 'The dog was very old, and did not seem particularly *viable*'" [my italics]. I, too, like the sentence but see little in the novel that is "warm and delightful about donnish life."

10. Annie Gottlieb, in "Three Hapless Heroines," *New York Times Book*

Review, 29 March 1981, 14, points out that "Ruth ends up back in London caring for her widowed invalid father in a manner more companionable than incestuous." Alix is proud of the fact that people used to take her father and her for lovers.

11. Frances's words remind us of Brookner's answering her interviewer's question: "Despite their subtlety and variations, all your books so far have been basically about love. Do you think you will go on writing about love?" She replies: "What else is there? All the rest is mere literature!" Guppy, "Art of Fiction," 169.

12. Cf. Duchêne, "Superior Melancholy": Nick is a "golden husk, drained by [his wife]."

13. Note this, for example, from Frances: "We are both rather old-fashioned, I suppose, and although our friendship is deep and sincere, we do not really subscribe to the women's guerrilla movement. I think we like to maintain a certain loyalty to the men who have, or have had, our love and affection; we regard ourselves in some way as being concerned with their honour. Ridiculous, really, when you come to think of it. I have learned that there is no reciprocity in these matters" (12).

14. Guppy, "Art of Fiction," 167–68.

15. Ibid., 167.

16. Nicholas Shrimpton, "Bond at 70," *New Statesman,* 22 May 1981, 21.

17. "*Look at Me,*" *Harper's* (July 1983), 75.

18. Guppy, "Art of Fiction," 148.

19. Ibid., 161–62.

20. Ibid., 161.

Chapter Five

1. Some critics have hated the novel, however—for example, Adam Mars-Jones, "Women Beware Women," *New York Review of Books,* 31 January 1985, 17, who points out that there was controversy when Brookner received the prize; Walter Clemons, "*Hotel du Lac,*" *Newsweek,* 25 February 1985, 87, who sees it as an "airless," "glacially perfect lit'ry novel, written by the numbers"; and Martha Bayles, "Romance à la Mode," *New Republic,* 25 March 1985, 38, who deems it a "Harlequin Romance for highbrows."

2. Guppy, "Art of Fiction," 151.

3. Brookner appears to call attention to her techniques, as previously with textual references to foils (and again in *Hotel du Lac,* 82). We are prepared, then, for an allusion to parody: "Just what I wanted, Edith reminded herself, but what she suddenly longed to do was to speak to David; the intrusion of a man into her consciousness, however *parodic,* had the painful effect of awakening her longing" (56; my italics).

4. The character is Daphne Dagnall in *A Few Green Leaves* (New York, 1981), 94.

5. As always, Brookner's opening is unusually effective, this time not the result of a startling idea or use of words so much as a word painting of the atmosphere: "seams of white on the far mountains, and on the cheerful uplands to the south a rising backdrop of apple trees, the fruit sparkling with emblematic significance" (7).

6. An example of the novel's playfulness is that her pen name, Vanessa Wilde, contains the same initials as the novelist Edith wants to look like. See John Gross, "*Hotel du Lac,*" *New York Times,* 22 January 1985, C17. Her agent, in one of the infrequent shifts of point of view from Edith, thinks that she "really does look remarkably Bloomsburian" (27). In spite of keeping Edith's point of view predominant, Brookner can also deftly manage a laugh at her expense. For example, Edith promotes her being compared with Woolf and waits eagerly for Mrs. Pusey to remember who it is that she reminds her of. When the answer finally comes, it is Princess Anne.

7. Mars-Jones, "Women Beware Women," points out that "there is some attempt to suggest that Edith writes in a sort of trance state" (18).

8. Mars-Jones in ibid. says that "a reader with any experience of romantic fiction is likely to realize that the letters are never sent" (18). See also Bayles, "Romance à la Mode," 37.

9. Edith's neighbor is named Penelope Milne, but nothing seems to be gained by examining either progenitor.

10. Mars-Jones, "Women Beware Women," points out that Edith "seems not to realize that she is under no obligation to use it in his absence" (18).

11. A variation on this relationship occurs in *The Misalliance,* where one of the "misalliances" of the title is Blanche's involvement with a young child who refuses to speak. One wonders if Brookner is not remembering some kindred episode in her own life or perhaps her own fragility as a child.

12. The description of Harold Webb—"A mild and scholarly man who looked like a country doctor, he disliked the more sociable aspects of his calling" (26)—is equally apt for Ned in *The Debut.*

13. She reminds us of Brookner's impassioned denunciation of "women's novels . . . written to a formula." Guppy, "Art of Fiction," 161. In that same interview (153), Brookner does a reprise of Edith on "The Tortoise and the Hare."

14. Critics have wondered if Brookner has not done more source pointing. Clemons, "*Hotel du Lac,*" 87, finds the book "an elegant facsimile of a novel that Elizabeth Bowen (*The Hotel*) and Christina Stead (*The Little Hotel*) have already done better." Sebastian Faulks, in "A Moral Tale," *Books and Bookmen* (September 1984), 18, points out that "one's heart sinks at the beginning to find that she has booked us into that old standby of English ironists, the hotel of disappointed gentility. Elizabeth Bowen has stayed here; Patrick Hamilton passed through on his way to Henley; and Terence Rattigan

was a pillar of the saloon bar." It is hard to imagine that Brookner would not have been familiar with at least some of these titles and authors and was deliberately calling her effort into comparison. She has dedicated *Hotel du Lac* to novelist Rosamond Lehmann. James Lasdun, in "Pre-Modern, Post Modernist: Recent Fiction," *Encounter* (February 1985), 42, sees a deliberate call for comparison with James: "A discreet reference, in the text, to Henry James confirms him as a model for both [style and subject matter]. The phrasing and cadencing of the sentences have a flavour that is strongly reminiscent of James—'It was to be supposed that . . . ,' 'an unsuspected note of glamour in the person of a lady of indeterminate age . . .'—as is the portrait painted, of a lady whose vision of happiness-as-the-Right-Marriage is ironically, almost tragically, undermined."

15. Guppy, "Art of Fiction," 154. Brookner also claims that her balking at the last minute and not letting Edith marry Mr. Neville is an indication of her not really being an imaginative writer (164).

16. Bayles, "Romance à la Mode," 37, thinks her an anorexic, but she is always eating cake. She certainly has nothing in common with Drabble's anorexic in *The Realms of Gold*.

17. Brookner seems to have an aversion to pink (because she is a redhead?). Frances (*Look at Me*) will not be caught, like Mrs. Halloran, in a housecoat "too young and too pink" (86). Blanche doubtless takes Elinor's being dressed in pink dungarees and anorak, with a pink bow in her hair, as evidence of her stepmother's failings (*The Misalliance,* 37). Heather, in *A Friend from England,* wears a suit "in the rather hideous pink that was so fashionable that year" to "go away in" after her ill-fated marriage (93).

18. Guppy, "Art of Fiction," 161.

Chapter Six

1. Mimi feels that "Dolly, well, Dolly is so beautiful that one can hardly expect her to conform to the rules that govern lesser people" (116).

2. In contrast to Barbara Pym and Margaret Drabble, Brookner does not often fill her novels with brand names and local color, though she can create interiors with a calculating eye. Notable examples are the furnishings of the Linton flat in *Look at Me,* described by Duchêne, "Superior Melancholy," as "1930s immemorabilia" and an "impeccable" "inventory," and various abodes of the Dorns.

3. Caryn James, "Snapshots of Lost Innocence," *New York Times Book Review,* 10 November 1985, 15.

4. Drabble, too, makes ironic use of dogs as the embodiment of the spirit of Old England. See my *Margaret Drabble* (Boston, 1986), 105–6.

5. Cf. Blanche Vernon, in *The Misalliance,* 99–100: "She thought of titanic roasts of beef, hecatombs of vegetables, puddings stuffed with fruit,

trembling custards." As a divorced woman with no one for whom to prepare
the standard fare of Old England, she feels herself a further failure.

    6. Brookner may have remembered this work, too, when she named
Professor Duplessis in *The Debut*. Marie Duplessis was the prototype of Margue-
rite Gautier, Dumas' heroine. If so, we see another interesting merging of
male and female.

    7. Robert E. Hosmer, Jr., "*Family and Friends*," *America*, 15 March
1986, 215.

    8. Cf. Susan Lardner, "Nostalgia," *New Yorker*, 10 March 1986, 121:
"*Family and Friends* opens with a quotation from Goethe . . . about the advan-
tages and disadvantages of social conventions and middle-class life. The epigraph indicates that *Family and Friends* may be taken as a kind of antidote to
Goethe's rendition of philosophical romanticism. 'Impropriety' is a better
word for the misbehavior Brookner describes than 'rebellion' or 'defiance,'
which is what Werther was up to. She does succeed in illustrating Goethe's
point about middle-class life—that there is not much excitement to it: an
artistic achievement that is less interesting to the reader than to the writer."

    9. For example, Hosmer, "*Family and Friends*," and A. N. Wilson,
"Significant Silences," *Times Literary Supplement*, 6 September 1985, 973.

    10. Critics do notice, however, its old-fashioned hue. James, "Snapshots
of Lost Innocence," finds "it . . . a relief that . . . the author has sent her
characters back to the past, where most Anita Brookner people might feel
more comfortable." "While the author looks backward, she focuses on the
breakdown of the old social codes and the forces that have led to her contemporary heroines' oddly dated notions of love and decorum" (15). See also D. J.
Enright, "Depositions," *New York Review of Books*, 5 December 1985, 37:
"These beautiful people, cosseted and cultivated, with their Mamas and Papas,
their schnapps and Madeira and marzipan cake, their music and dancing, their
finishing schools in Switzerland, their cigars and family businesses, seem
rather to be inmates of Marienbad or Vienna around the turn of the century."

    11. For example, Mimi and Betty in their pre-Raphelite dresses (16),
Frederick in the stance of the Apollo Belvedere (17), Betty looking like a
painting by Foujita (40) and Mimi like Rossetti's "Beata Beatrix" (70), and
Evie as too viable to be an oil painting (74).

    12. See James, "Snapshots of Lost Innocence," 15: "She means her charac-
ters to be types, yet pulls off the difficult balancing act of showing the individuals behind their conventional postures of ladies' man or dutiful daughter."

    13. This undeveloped narrator frustrates some critics, for example, ibid.:
"Why doesn't the narrative voice describing these few photographs develop
any persona at all?".

    14. Enright, "Depositions," 37. Enright is also relieved "to discover a
novel with Jewish characters but no Holocaust."

    15. Phoebe-Lou Adams, "Brief Reviews," *Atlantic* (November 1985),
144.

16. Enright, "Deposition," 37.
17. Ibid.

Chapter Seven

1. The title of the original British version was *A Misalliance.*

2. Mme de Staël is an excellent choice for Blanche, for, as Brookner says of her in "Corinne and Her *Coups de Foudre,*" *Times Literary Supplement,* 14 March 1980, 287, "It was this extraordinary woman's fate to be a laughing stock." Much the same thing could be said of Blanche. Mme de Staël was also involved with Benjamin Constant, whose novel *Adolphe* Kitty Maule teaches in *Providence.*

3. Guppy, "Art of Fiction," 150–51.

4. On the migraine, see Adrianne Blue, *Times Literary Supplement,* 29 August 1986, 112: "The best realised scene in this short novel is the description of the migraine Blanche gets. . . . The novel shows how Blanche comes to terms with the hole Bertie's absence has made in the fabric of her life. The migraine works exquisitely as a scene and as a symbol of this depressed heroine's woes, and as a device for allowing more characters into her empty life, thereby supplying the mild suspense that precedes the bittersweet ending, which is very clever."

5. See also p. 108 for another use of *valid* in a context of children: "Numbly she [Blanche] acknowledged the fact that all her efforts led towards sadness. For that reason she had no way of knowing whether or not they were *valid.* She supposed her sadness to be a matter of temperament or rather an accident of birth, as if, in some gigantic lottery, it had been decided that she were to be denied the enjoyment of her own free will. And the irony of it was that she had been unaware of this fact until she was middle-aged. As a child, like all children, she had felt that the world was as much hers as anybody else's; and as a grown woman she had had no reason to doubt her happy state. It was only recently that the truth had begun to become clear to her, as if only just coming into focus. It was now that she saw the superior freedom of others."

6. Cf.: "And then I saw the pattern. The pattern is plain for all to see. One visit to the National Gallery would convince you, if you were in any doubt. There they all are, the good and the indifferent. I incline to think that there *are* no bad. Indifference to the good is all that is needed" (171).

7. Michiko Kakutani, "Books of *The Times,*" *New York Times,* 25 March 1987, C23, sees a Jamesian interplay in *The Misalliance* between innocence and sophistication although "Miss Brookner's aims . . . are considerably more modest: she simply wants to use the dichotomy as an explanation for the fact that some women are more successful than others in the departments of sex and romance."

8. Guppy, "Art of Fiction," 165–66.

9. Cf. Merle Rubin, *Christian Science Monitor*, 18 June 1987, 26, who finds Blanche "the most constructively self-critical woman Brookner has portrayed thus far."

Chapter Eight

1. "The curious name of Sandberg was conferred on them by some slightly complicated ancestry: there was a Danish grandfather, apparently, as well as an Irish grandmother, or possibly two. . . . At the same time, the long periods spent in Spain or Portugal had resulted in a very slight blurring of the sibilants in their speech, more noticeable when father and son spoke to each other than when they spoke to the rest of us. It was like a little code between them, rather charming" (49).

2. The same blending of minor characters as in *Family and Friends* occurs, too, as well as the appearance of wedding photographs (93), important for Rachel's assessment of the marriage between Heather and Michael (if lacking in the expansive treatment of that earlier book) and suggesting a similar German background. Rachel finds the sisters and brothers-in-law "less interesting because more worldly" (23) and cannot distinguish the latter: they are "amiable, rather supine men, as men tend to be when married to nervous critical women, and their task in life was to calm their wives down" (23). Brookner cleverly reveals the loss of individuality without having to describe it: " 'Well, we shall know who to come to,' said either Gerald or Lawrence . . . , while either Lawrence or Gerald added, 'Perhaps you could send us some of the literature' " (45).

3. Other examples of Rachel's literary references include her rejection of Stendhal (129, 132) and her accusation that Heather has mastered Joyce's "desiderata for an artist's life"—"silence, exile, and cunning" (147).

4. Wealth and privilege renounced are a strong theme in Drabble's *The Needle's Eye,* and we have to suspect an allusion to it in Rachel's "I had never known anyone so scandalously rich before, and I wanted to see if it had changed them. I imagined that the possession of wealth made itself known through some kind of stigmata: I foresaw difficulties in getting through *the eye of a needle,* and wondered if the *strain would show*" (11; my italics). Dorrie and Oscar are uncomfortable with their wealth, but Brookner introduces a factor not in Drabble—age: "Although they had no reason to be unhappy, they were not altogether happy, and they were too innocent to recognize their condition as pertaining to age rather than to substance. The time of reckoning was upon them: if they had ever wished for anything, they now realized that life had moved them on from logical fulfillment of those wishes" (16–17). Again we have the impression that Brookner rather than Rachel (who is, after all, only thirty-two) is making this observation. Similarly when Rachel gets the flu, she becomes "like an old woman" (96), and much is made of the signs of aging in the still-beautiful Dorrie and in men in general (90).

5. "It would be nice to be free. Freedom was not really a viable proposition, although an illusion of freedom—and it nearly always is an illusion—came to me in dreams, those same dreams in which I loved and drowned" (88).

6. As usual, sex is present in Brookner primarily as something that happens offstage in the ironically otherwise carefully dissected lives of the main characters. Particularly in *Look at Me* and *A Friend from England*, it is a major influence on the heroines. Here Brookner recognizes its pervasiveness as the concern of the aunts to get Heather married is seen as "not devoid of a certain prurience, the prurience that some ageing women feel when excluded from the sexual odysseys of the young" (30).

7. "Of course, I knew all about fathers and daughters and what they are supposed to feel for each other. Heather's lack of ardour in acknowledging the fact that she had met someone may have been inspired by the desire to spare her father embarrassment or discomfort. She was, as I have said shrewd. Maybe this toneless and passionless announcement was part of her enlightened daughterliness" (39–40). On the other hand, Oscar and Dorrie look so remarkably alike that Rachel originally mistook them for brother and sister (9).

8. Brookner has used the term *fugue* in a similar way in *The Misalliance* (122).

9. Brookner makes the point that all humans, male and female, are capable of wanting contrast in their lives. Rachel and Robin's partner, Eileen Somers, "a widow with two undergraduate sons, has a side-line in free-fall parachuting. Her late husband was a Wing-Commander in the Royal Air Force, and she feels that in this way she can keep in touch with him. Eccentricities abound in the most orthodox, the most humdrum of lives" (66).

10. Not a don, Rachel nonetheless obviously knows about art as about literature. She thinks that Heather looks like the bride in a Breughel painting (47) and has a "Gioconda-like smile" (51). Dorrie, with her bandaged ear, looks like Van Gogh and has painted watercolors in her time (136). With irony, Brookner has Rachel remember Bosch's painting, alluded to also in *Hotel du Lac*, in recording that "Heather's flat was not the *garden of earthly delights* that Dorrie's house had been to me" (99; my italics). More to the point, it is not the sexual "garden of earthly delights" that it should be for the pair just back from their honeymoon.

11. Guppy, "Art of Fiction," 166–67.

Selected Bibliography

Primary Works

Novels

A Start in Life. London: Jonathan Cape, Ltd., 1981; *The Debut.* New York: Linden Press/Simon and Schuster, 1981.
Providence. London: Jonathan Cape, Ltd., 1982; New York: Pantheon Books, 1982.
Look at Me. London: Jonathan Cape, Ltd., 1983; New York: Pantheon Books, 1983.
Hotel du Lac. London: Jonathan Cape, Ltd., 1984; New York: Pantheon Books, 1984.
Family and Friends. London: Jonathan Cape, Ltd., 1985; New York: Pantheon Books, 1985.
A Misalliance. London: Jonathan Cape, Ltd., 1986; *The Misalliance.* New York: Pantheon Books, 1986.
A Friend from England. London: Jonathan Cape, Ltd., 1987; New York: Pantheon Books, 1987.

Nonfiction

Watteau. Feltham: Hamlyn Publishing Group Ltd., 1967.
The Genius of the Future: Studies in French Art Criticism [Diderot, Stendhal, Baudelaire, Zola, The Brothers Goncourt, and Huysmans]. London and New York: Phaidon, 1971.
Greuze: The Rise and Fall of an Eighteenth-Century Phenomenon. London: Paul Elek Limited, 1972; Greenwich, Conn.: New York Graphic Society Ltd., 1972.
Jacques-Louis David: A Personal Interpretation. Lecture on Aspects of Art. Henriette Hertz Trust of the British Academy, 1974; London: Oxford University Press, 1974.
"Rousseau and the Social Contract." *Times Literary Supplement,* 8 February 1980, 149.
"Corinne and Her *Coups de Foudre.*" *Times Literary Supplement,* 14 March 1980, 287.
"The Bibliothèque Nationale." *Times Literary Supplement,* 5 October 1984, 26.

Secondary Works

Articles

Adams, Phoebe-Lou. "Brief Reviews." *Atlantic* (November 1985), 143–44.
Anon. Introduction to "Anita Brookner: *Hotel du Lac.*" *Contemporary Literary Criticism Yearbook* 34 (1984), 136–43. Quotes the novelist on her literary influences, family and life, and reasons for starting to write fiction.
Anon. "Briefly Noted." *New Yorker,* 18 May 1987, 115–20. Includes a review of *The Misalliance.* Cites similarities to Jane Austen.
Bayles, Martha. "Romance à la Mode." *New Republic,* 25 March 1985, 37–38. Sees *Hotel du Lac* as a "comedy of manners, capturing a peculiar mode of frustration, which occurs whenever the English encounter one another in a foreign place"; calls it a "Harlequin Romance for high-brows."
Blue, Adrianne. "Floral Print." *New Statesman,* 22 August 1986, 26. A review of *The Misalliance* arguing that Brookner is read by feminists but is not a feminist and that, in fact, "What Brookner is cooking up is Mills & Boon for bluestockings." Sees the best scene in *The Misalliance* as the migraine; finds that the beginning fails.
Cantwell, Mary. "Not Hungry Enough." *New York Times Book Review,* 22 May 1983, 14. A review of *Look at Me* seeing it as "a horror story about monsters and their victims told in exceptionally elegant prose."
Clemons, Walter. "*Hotel du Lac.*" *Newsweek,* 25 February 1985, 87. "An elegant facsimile of a novel that Elizabeth Bowen (*The Hotel*) and Christina Stead (*The Little Hotel*) have already done better."
Cole, Diane. "Travels of the Mind." *Ms.* (June 1985), 63. "If you're a Noel Coward fan, no doubt you'll find it (*Hotel du Lac*) amusing and fun, but it left me as dissatisfied as one of those creaky well-made British stage plays from the 1930s: yes, the insights, the dialogue, the character portraits are all quite charming, but what lies beneath the witty surface, the sparkling veneer?"
Craig, Patricia. "On Not Being Overwhelmed." *Times Literary Supplement,* 29 August 1986, 932. Sees *The Misalliance* as "a civilized look at contemporary disorder, and a wonderfully poised and pointed examination of the wrong turning." Good on the oppositions that thread Brookner novels.
Duchêne, Anne. "Superior Melancholy." *Times Literary Supplement,* 25 March 1983, 289. A review of *Look at Me* seeing it as "A study in the kind of loneliness that is self-induced and self-destructive"; "The book's virtue is in making one want to debate it. It is impossible to read it passively."
Eberstadt, Fernanda. "Good Works and Bad Lovers." *New York Times Book Review,* 29 March 1987, 10. Argues that *The Misalliance* displays Brookner's "formidable gifts as a psychologist of the wounded woman's heart" and that her weaknesses are her tendency to explain rather than show

and the disappointing "pagans." Nonetheless, concludes that Brookner deserves her reputation as one of the finest novelists of her generation.

Enright, D. J. "Depositions." *New York Review of Books,* 5 December 1985, 35–37. Includes a review of *Family and Friends* finding the prose style impeccable but the novel flawed by characters being described entirely from the outside; finds the atmosphere "almost claustrophobic." Assesses the book as one to be admired rather than enjoyed.

Epstein, Julia. "Images of Melancholy." *Washington Post,* 24 July 1983, 6. Sees *Look at Me* as a "nearly impossible achievement, a novel about emptiness and vacancy"; argues that it is also about writing a novel, but that Brookner alters the frame "so that her subject is not the writing but the gathering and absorbing and sifting of quotidian detail." Concludes that Brookner achieves what Flaubert once tried to do: write "a book about nothing."

Faulks, Sebastian. "A Moral Tale." *Books and Bookmen* (September 1984), 18. Includes a review of *Hotel du Lac.* Posits that, at the end, Brookner and Edith Hope "both make the right choice and they do so in a way that not only redeems the novel from its unoriginality" but moved the reviewer to tears.

Gates, David. "Footnotes." *Newsweek,* 30 March 1987, 69. Includes a review of *The Misalliance* arguing that the title refers to Blanche's friendship with Sally. Sees the "most daring move" saved for the last page and finds that it "realigns the novel into a pleasing yet unsettling symmetry."

Gies, Judith. "An Anachronism in Love." *New York Times Book Review,* 18 March 1984, 17. A review of *Providence* arguing that Brookner's protagonists share "a tragicomic ambivalence toward the moral standards and the expectations we learn from books." States that whereas Pym's women always have "the comforts of the parish jumble sale," Kitty is an anachronism whose "future will not be cozy." Concludes that she is "not so much a real woman as a symbol of the disappointed child in all of us."

Glastonbury, Marion. "Sentimental Education." *New Statesman,* 14 May 1982, 25. Includes a review of *Providence* arguing that Maurice "remains . . . part-icon and part-knitting pattern: a pair of ivory ears over a cashmere pullover." Concludes that Brookner provides excellent portraits of age.

Gottlieb, Annie. "Three Hapless Heroines." *New York Times Book Review,* 29 March 1981, 14–15. Includes a review of *The Debut* that sees the novel dealing with failure; finds Ruth "a renunciant by fate or nature"; notices the portrait of Ruth's mother and the relationship between Ruth and her father.

Greenland, Colin. "Mists of Time." *New Statesman,* 6 September 1985, 30. Includes a review of *Family and Friends* that sees Brookner preserving "an even-handed neutrality of tone, a kind of well-bred Bloomsburyish murmur. Outside, barely remarked, the Second World War slips by."

Gross, John. *"Hotel du Lac." New York Times,* 22 January 1985, C17. Finds novel "satisfyingly urbane"; sees Brookner as "one of the finest novelists of her generation."

Guppy, Shusha. "The Art of Fiction XCVIII: Anita Brookner." *Paris Review* 29 (1987), 147–69. One of the few interviews with Brookner. Some biographical details, how her life has influenced her writing, literary influences on her, why she started writing, how she writes, her view of feminism, her observations about the novels.

Harvey, Stephen. *"Look at Me." Village Voice,* 5 July 1983, 46. Assesses the overuse of *I.* "Schematic, self-conscious fiction which is a substitute for literature."

Helgesen, Sally. "Anita Brookner's Damaged Goods." *Village Voice,* 22 January, 1985, 43–44. Review of *Hotel du Lac* that suggests Brookner's novels are about the "transformation of frightened and angry girls" into "competent and confident women"; concludes that the Brookner heroine becomes a feminist "by learning to be a lady."

Hosmer, Robert E., Jr. *"Family and Friends." America,* 15 March 1986, 215–16. Finds the novel the best of the first four and sees the best scene as immediately after Sofka's death.

James, Caryn. "Snapshots of Lost Innocence." *New York Times Book Review,* 10 November 1985, 15. A review of *Family and Friends* that suggests the novel shows Brookner "taking control of the genre she has inherited from Jane Austen and Barbara Pym."

Jebb, Julian. "Unblinking." *Spectator,* 22 September 1984, 26–27. A review of *Hotel du Lac:* "A classic, a book which will be read with pleasure a hundred years from now." Argues that Brookner may be indebted to the classical French romances of the nineteenth century, but that no other piece of modern fiction has "the extraordinary blend of wit, seriousness and an unassuming attitude to philosophy."

Jones, Robert. "Romancing the Novel." *Commonweal,* 20 September 1985, 502–3. A review of *Hotel du Lac* arguing that the novel seems "humorless to the point of perversity," with "stock characters" and "lifeless prose." "If [Brookner] has a parallel in English literature, we should not look to Virginia Woolf, but to Mrs. Humphrey Ward, that purveyor of countless volumes of pretentious Victorian entertainments." States that the novel has a "bogus quality" from Brookner's attempt to link herself with great writers by echo and reference and "panders to the sentimentality of every undergraduate majoring in English literature." Concludes that Brookner feels no different about writing than "Vivienne Wilde" [*sic*].

Jordan, Elaine. "Travelling." *London Review of Books,* 21 April–4 May 1983, 22–23. Sees *Look at Me* as "not a novel of scenes but a meditation on experience in the French tradition." Sees a problem in "how far Frances is presented ironically."

Kakutani, Michiko. "Books of *The Times.*" *New York Times,* 25 March 1987, C23. Compares Blanche of *The Misalliance* with Blanche DuBois in *A Streetcar Named Desire,* arguing that what is different about this Brookner novel is the "expertly rendered" conclusion, suggesting the "promise of new life" and "redemption."

————. "Genteel Predators." *New York Times,* 20 February 1988, 16. A review of *A Friend from England* finding Rachel an unreliable narrator who misrepresents others and deludes herself; cites more repetitious personalities. Concludes that Brookner's tendency is to "explain, rather than dramatize, to tell rather than show."

Kearns, Kathleen. "Brief Reviews." *New Republic,* 26 March 1984, 39–40. Finds *Providence* "full of missed signals" and feels that sometimes it is "difficult to distinguish Brookner's perspective from Kitty's." "An uncomfortable sense emerges that Brookner wants to be critical of her tiresome heroine, even make fun of her, but can't quite bring herself to do it."

Lardner, Susan. "Books: Nostalgia." *New Yorker,* 10 March 1986, 121–22. A review of *Family and Friends.* "Slow motion and equanimity muffle the force even of illicit love affairs and disappointed hopes; the present-tense narrative has a congealing effect. Although that particular prewar period is still within reach of memory for some, the way Brookner tells it it is ancient history."

Lasdun, James. "Pre-Modern, Post-Modernist: Recent Fiction." *Encounter,* February 1985, 42, 44–47. Includes a review of *Hotel du Lac;* finds that "on its own terms . . . [the novel] comes as close to a kind of flawlessness as it is possible to imagine in a novel written today." Sees Henry James as the model for both style and subject matter.

Lee, Hermione. "Cleopatra's Way." *Observer,* 9 September 1984, 22. A review of *Hotel du Lac;* sees the novel written with "a beautiful grave formality"; says it "catches at the heart" but raises a doubt: "The 'Brookner' hallmarks—a twilit, dreamlike inwardness, an austerely circumscribed subject-matter, an infinite melancholy—become, perhaps, a little shadowy and self-shadowing."

————. "Drowning Tastefully in the Dark." *Los Angeles Times,* 20 March 1988, 2, 12. A review of *A Friend from England* finding it "comfortless and discomforting." "Late James hangs, somewhat stiflingly, over the whole novel." Argues that Brookner has been consistently misread and is actually "an obsessive, clinical, severely disenchanted writer."

McRobbie, Angela. "Fine Disorder." *New Statesman,* 7 September 1984, 32, 34. Includes a review of *Hotel du Lac* that finds the novel interesting for "the debt it owes to its lower generic equivalent, the pulp romance. The slow sorrow with life which finds temporary release in the strong-jawed hero is here displaced into a more upmarket world."

Mars-Jones, Adam. "Women Beware Women." *New York Times Book Review,* 31 January 1985, 17–19. Includes a review of *Hotel du Lac* suggesting that the novel's success depends on Edith's "being convincingly vulnerable" and that the novel is "divided between narcissism and self-mortification, between wallowing and astringency; the curious combination of urges that might lead a person, say, to take an ice-cold bubble bath."

Plante, David. "They Won Their Life on the Football Pools." *New York Times Book Review,* 20 March 1988, 10–11. A review of *A Friend from England* that sees the novel as typical Brookner fare in the "foreignness" of the heroine and the bourgeois values she observes; a "delicate portrait of a brave woman who suffers the loss of the world."

Prescott, Peter A. "The Last Romantic." *Newsweek,* 27 February 1984, 71. Argues that *Providence* lacks action and is "Woman's Desperate Lot, Episode 7,291" and that Kitty never sees that "she herself is the last of the alienated Romantics" in love with the standard "male bounder" of the genre, as Brookner makes sure the reader knows. Concludes that the book "is high-class garbage, the kind they put out in the alley behind Claridge's. It should please a lot of educated women who wouldn't dream of reading Rosemary Rogers."

Roston, Annie. "*Look at Me.*" *Harper's* (July 1983), 75. Finds that the book has a special kind of suspense: "Frances, with her deadpan manner, is so peculiar that she intrigues the reader." A "remarkably fresh novel."

Rubin, Merle. "Anita Brookner's Novels: Old Moral Choices without the Old Rhetoric" and "Casting Moral Puzzles: A Novelist on Her Craft." *Christian Science Monitor,* 1 March 1985, B3. The first article is a review of *Hotel du Lac* that, examining all of the novels, finds growth in the "sheer beauty" of Brookner's prose and cites the author's ability as "a master artist to keep discovering new patterns and nuances in the same picture." Sees the theme of *Hotel du Lac* as "the great Romantic theme of hope in the face of despair." The second piece is particularly important for Brookner's own comment on her fiction (based on a telephone interview), including her belief that its most important feature "is its capacity to present people in the process of making choices."

———. "Latest Brookner Novel Follows a Character in Search of Herself." *Christian Science Monitor,* 18 June 1987, 26. Finds the writing in *The Misalliance* "as ever" "exquisite." Sees Blanche as "the most constructively self-critical" Brookner woman and says that she finds a way "beyond the artificial antitheses of egoism and altruism, self-assertion and self-denial."

Schofield, Mary Anne. "Spinster's Fare: Rites of Passage in Anita Brookner's Fiction." In *Cooking by the Book: Food in Literature and Culture.* Edited by Mary Anne Schofield. Bowling Green, Ohio: Popular Culture Press, in press. An excellent treatment of Brookner's use of food and food imagery as a principal way of expressing the problems of female being and selfhood.

Sheppard, R. Z. "Ashes of Envy." *Time,* 21 March 1988, 76, 78. A review of *A Friend from England.* Sees Brookner "as hard-boiled as any writer of detective fiction." Concludes that Rachel is self-deceived about what is real.

Shrimpton, Nicholas. "Bond at 70." *New Statesman,* 22 May 1981, 21. Includes a review of *A Start in Life:* "The sort of book which gives feminist writing a good name." About the sacrifice of daughters to elderly parents. The craftsmanship is "almost too sedulous."

Taliaferro, Frances. "Fiction." *Harper's* (February 1984), 75–76. A review of *Providence* that sums the achievement of the first three novels: "politely agoraphobic works" "for a disciplined sensibility," in all of which "femininity is lodged useless." "*Providence* has many of the Brooknerian virtues that distinguish the other two novels: elegant prose, ironic humor, a delicate astuteness about character, and a fine sensitivity to the oddities of various social groups," plus "painterly attention to detail" and a "rich bookishness." Concludes, however, that *Providence* is a short story stretched too far.

Taubman, Robert. "Submission." *London Review of Books,* 20 May–2 June 1982, 18–19. Sees *Providence* as Brookner's second novel about "the subjugation and defeat of an intelligent heroine." Asks why Brookner has used so much "delicacy and irony" on situations she "has planned from the start will come to nothing."

Tyler, Anne. "A Solitary Life Is Still Worth Living." *New York Times Book Review,* 3 February 1985, 1, 31. A review of *Hotel du Lac* finding it Brookner's "most absorbing novel." Contrasts Pym and Brookner.

Wilson, A. N. "Significant Silences." *Times Literary Supplement,* 6 September 1985, 973. Finds *Family and Friends* the best of Brookner's novels to date primarily because of the "brilliance" with which the "chronicle problem" is resolved. Compares Brookner and Ivy Compton-Burnett.

Index

Ackroyd, Peter, 5
Aesop, 58
Anderson, Sherwood. "Death in the
    Woods," 11
Anne, Princess, 150n6
Arnold, Matthew, 82

Balzac, Honoré de, 5, 15, 26; *Eugénie
    Grandet,* 3, 8, 10, 11, 12, 13, 14,
    16, 17, 18, 19, 22, 144n4
Baudelaire, 4
Bellow, Saul, 6
Berlin, Isaiah, 5
Bibliothèque Nationale, 4, 7, 10
Born, Edith de, 5
Bosch, Hieronymus, 57, 155n10
Bowen, Elizabeth, 150–51n14
Breughel, Pieter, 155n10
BROOKNER, Anita, appearance, 4,
    143–44n13; art in the novels,
    102–3, 114, 148n7, 152n11,
    155n10; articles and reviews, 7;
    autobiographical details in the nov-
    els, 1, 2–3, 6, 12, 14, 16–17, 20,
    36, 42, 92, 108, 145n8, 145n1;
    background, 2; biblical imagery,
    123–24; biographical information
    on, 1–7, 92, 140, 143n2, 145n12,
    145n13, 145n2, 146–47n11;
    Booker-McConnell Prize for Fic-
    tion, 7, 55, 140, 149n1; and art,
    3, 4; and differences between criti-
    cism and fiction, 5; and women's
    novels 150n13; the characters beset
    by contradictions, 20, 45; the char-
    acters' condescension, 147n16; the
    characters' relation to literature,
    11–15, 22–29, 38, 79–80, 99–
    100, 122–29, 140–41, 154n3;
    children and mothers in the novels,
    69–74, 100, 105–9, 128, 137–

39; differences between author and
    characters, 6; domestics in the nov-
    els, 114; education, 3; family influ-
    ence on, 2, 92; feminist and quasi-
    feminist concerns, 50–53, 89, 94,
    99, 105, 111, 129–36, 149n13;
    food imagery, 34, 36, 144n1,
    147n22, 151n16, 151–52n5;
    "golden" figures in the novels, 9,
    10, 13, 16, 23, 24, 27, 35, 36,
    80, 83, 138, 149n12; heroines'
    view of men and love, 9, 14–15,
    21, 24, 26, 73, 89, 95, 127–28,
    131, 140, 149n11; home of, 6; hu-
    mor and playfulness in the novels,
    148n4, 150n6; irony, 56, 86, 87,
    91, 102, 114, 115, 122, 137; lu-
    cidity as a writer, 7; male characters
    and view of men, 50–53, 60, 63–
    64, 68, 74–83, 91–92, 96–98,
    109, 113, 116, 134–35, 144n2;
    merging of literal and figural, 129,
    137, 145n9; openings of the novels
    150n5; opposing types in the novels
    and extremes of the continuum, 13,
    15, 25, 26–27, 28, 29–33, 38,
    41, 45, 47, 68, 74, 77, 81, 83–
    91, 95–105, 106, 108, 113, 120,
    129, 130, 131, 137, 146n6; read-
    ing, 5; recurrent terms in the nov-
    els, 18, 27, 37, 43, 73, 75, 81,
    85, 91, 97, 105, 106, 107, 114,
    129, 148n9, 153n5, 155n8; recur-
    rent themes and materials in the
    novels, 9, 11, 12, 13, 14, 20, 21,
    22, 31, 33, 35–36, 39, 40, 41,
    45, 47, 48, 54, 55, 56, 57, 58,
    60, 61, 63, 64, 65, 68–69, 73,
    74, 80, 81, 89, 95, 98, 99, 100,
    102, 103, 114, 115, 117–22, 128,
    132, 134, 137, 138, 145n3,

Gallant, Mavis, 5
Goethe, Johann Wolfgang von: *Sorrows of Young Werther,* 5, 91, 103, 152n8
Gogh, Vincent Willem Van, 155n10
Goncourt, the Brothers, 4

Hamilton, Patrick, 150–51n14
Hercules, 95, 107
Heyer, Georgette, 15
Hitchcock, Alfred, 147n15
Huysmans, Joris-Karl, 4

James, Henry, 5, 15, 46, 114, 144n18, 150–51n14, 153n7; *The Ambassadors,* 31, 81; "The Beast in the Jungle," 16, 135
Jameson, Storm, 5
Joyce, James, 154n3

Kleist, Heinrich von, 5

Lehmann, Rosamond, 5, 150–51n14
Leonardo Da Vinci, 155n10
Lurie, Allison, 6

Mortimer, John, 148n4

Nietzsche, Friedrich Wilhelm, 57

Plato, 95, 101, 109
Prescott, William H.: *The Conquest of Peru,* 78
Proust, Marcel, 5
Puccini, Giacomo: *La Bohème,* 125
Pym, Barbara, 6, 9, 16, 24, 33, 39, 48,

55, 60, 63, 64, 93, 95, 111–12, 129, 146n7, 151n2; *A Few Green Leaves,* 150n4
Quéffelec, Yann, 5

Rattigan, Terence, 150–51n14
Rhys, Jean, 5
Rossetti, Dante Gabriel, 89
Roth, Philip, 5
Rousseau, Jean-Jacques, 7

Sartre, Jean-Paul, 145n13
Shakespeare, William, 60, 79, 131
Sleeping Beauty, 104, 109
Staël, Mme de, 7, 99, 153n2
Stead, Christiana, 145n14, 150–51n14
Stendhal (Henri Beyle), 4, 5, 154n3

Taylor, Elizabeth, 5
Templeton, Edith, 5
Tennyson, Alfred Lord: "The Lady of Shalott," 89
Tolstoy, Leo: *Anna Karenina,* 12, 51, 145n7
Trollope, Anthony, 5

Voltaire (François-Marie Arouet): *Candide,* 57

Wharton, Edith, 5
Woolf, Virginia, 54, 55, 66, 150n6
Wordsworth, William, 99, 147n14

Zola, Émile, 4, 5